GARDENING
ALL YOU NEED TO KNOW

ACKNOWLEDGEMENTS

To Alex *and* Alex,
Liz and Anne,
Sara, Julia and John

Also in the Right Way series

Vegetable Growing Month by Month
Vegetable, Fruit and Herb Growing in Small Spaces
The Essential Allotment Guide

Uniform with this book

GARDENING

ALL YOU NEED
TO KNOW

Richard Rosenfeld

RIGHT WAY

Constable & Robinson Ltd
3 The Lanchesters
162 Fulham Palace Road
London W6 9ER
www.constablerobinson.com

First published by Right Way, an imprint of
Constable & Robinson, 2010

A copy of the British Library Cataloguing in Publication Data
is available from the British Library

ISBN: 978-0-7160-2236-7

Printed and bound in the EU

1 3 5 7 9 10 8 6 4 2

CONTENTS

1

THE GARDEN'S ENGINE – THE SOIL

Flannery O'Connor said that to write fiction you need a dash of "calculated stupidity". Spot on. And the same with gardening. Except, and this is where everything starts, the goal is fizzing, nutritious soil. Oxygenated, fertile, crumbly.

Soil isn't inert, fixed and preserved. Millions of years ago it was mainly rock; now it's alive, creating new plant food. A potent mix of minerals and organic matter. Living organisms in the soil react with the dead, generating a multitude of chemicals. And the soil is a biological powerhouse, booming with millions of single-celled bacteria in every single spoonful. Think of it as a great quivering foetus needing to be fed and pampered on an Olympic scale; the more organic material you fork in, the better. Put your ear to the ground and you can virtually hear it belch.

Good soil does three things. It feeds plants with ever-changing levels of oxygen, nutrients and water, it protects the roots from the fiercest summer heat and winter cold, and it provides the anchorage, locking plants in the ground. And what no one seems to realize is that most roots are right beneath your feet, in the top 10–15cm (4–6in) of soil. They rarely plunge any deeper. They're not racing to the centre of the earth. Which begs the question, why doesn't the topsoil resemble the deep-below? Because what you can poke and finger and smell is largely foreign – an import – soil which has been dumped here from all over the place by ancient glaciers and the wind. That's why you might have a mix of radically different kinds of soil in your garden, dumped in different places.

Keeping the soil in good shape

Good soil is the Holy Of Holies. Don't muck it around. Feed it. Here are the rules.

Add organic matter

Whenever you plant, add organic matter (composted bark, garden compost, leafmould, mushroom compost or well-rotted manure that's at least six months old) to the planting hole and that's like giving the soil an upgrade. If you want to use slow-release organics the choice includes (a) pelleted poultry manure, (b) bonemeal, (c) hoof and horn, (d) blood, fish and bone – the top choice – and (e) seaweed meal. They release nutrients which support both the plants and soil organisms, and they're incredibly useful when you're adding the likes of leafmould because that hardly has any nutrients.

Organic matter also makes a fantastic mulch in late autumn (insulating plants' roots when it's viciously cold) and/or in early spring. Dollop it across every patch of soil, a rollicking 8cm (3in) thick, keeping it clear of the stems. Do this after a night of heavy rain and it'll lock the moisture in the ground, stopping it from quickly evaporating, and initially cuts down on the amount of watering you've got to do. Mulching also hammers annual weeds by stopping the seeds getting any light and bursting into growth though it certainly won't kill existing ones (and that's why you should always weed *before* you mulch). Mulching – and this is the best bit – also improves the soil texture because the mulch eventually gets dragged down by worms. They're insatiable churners.

Make your own compost

There are two basic kinds, and the easiest is leafmould. When standing under a tree – and the remorseless point of a tree is to muscle up that thumping storm of leaves weighing maybe 1 ton to the light, which is why trees in tropical jungles need tall, thin, agile, 4-minute-a-mile trunks because they've got to leg it through the canopy to get to the sun as quickly as possible – look up at all those leaves and say to yourself "Compost", like Homer Simpson dribbling over a doughnut. All those flapping up-there leaves will soon be down here, under your feet, giving you a crumbly, open soil. And it's not just deciduous trees which drop leaves; so do evergreens.

The quickest way to make the autumn leaves vanish is to hoover them up in the lawnmower. In fact shredding them with grass clippings is a good(ish) thing because that boosts their low nutrient levels, but that isn't the point. Using compost is like putting yeast in bread. It "activates". It conditions and improves the soil. But get rid of any tough, thick leaves and chuck them in your main compost heap (see below) because they take so long to rot down. Now pack all the leaves you are keeping into black bin bags, quickly spray inside with water and then tie up the top and stab the sides to let in air. That's it. Stack them away in a cool place for 12–16 months. The longer you leave them, the crumblier the end product. Alternatively, create a permanent open container using four stout posts about waist high hammered in the ground, with nailed up chicken wire for the walls, and more chicken wire for the lid, and let the leaves rot down in there *but* it will take much longer. (See Fig. 1 overleaf.)

The main garden compost heap has more nutrients and is terrific at opening up the soil – making it crumblier – which is essential when the ground is gunky, lumpy and heavy. Use anything from grass clippings and kitchen scraps (eg vegetable peelings and tea leaves) to annual weeds, paper and cardboard. Avoid meat because you'll get rats, diseased

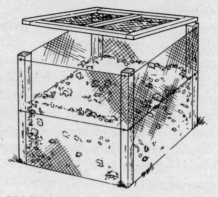

Fig. 1. A DIY container for leaves to make leafmould.

plants, the seedheads of weeds and anything that has been doused with weedkiller. The key rules are, first, buy a compost bin (OK) or make a wooden one (go for it). Stand it in the sun on well-drained soil, not tarmac. You want worms yo-yoing in and out, up-down, aerating, churning.

For the DIY kind (Fig. 2), make three walls about waist high from airy wooden slats nailed to stout posts, but the front wall isn't fixed in place because you need to remove it to get in and turn over the pile, letting in oxygen. Or make the walls from wooden pallets from a builder's yard. Then you'll need a lid to keep the compost dry and retain the heat. In both cases, that's the ready-made and DIY kind, the bigger the bin the better and, if you've got room, aim for three (yes, *three*) with the first being the current pile, the second an old pile that's composting away and nearly ready to use, and the third with the finished compost that's being used right now.

Fill the heap with about 35–40 per cent of nitrogen-high kitchen waste, weeds and grass clippings, etc, with the rest being made up of carbon-high paper, ripped up cardboard or dead leaves. Spray the heap in dry weather, make sure there's always a good mix of ingredients, and wait from nine months (six if you're lucky) to two years to get a luscious, dark brown crumbly texture with a rich sweet earthy pong. The

Fig. 2. A DIY compost bin.

maximum inner temperature of a heap can hit 70°C (158°F).
If you're buying a bin, you'll need 350 litres plus. Nothing
smaller.

Never stand on the soil
Never stand on the soil, especially when it's wet. That's like
punching a piece of bread dough, punching out the air. You'll
ruin the soil's texture. What you want is a loose, crumbly,
open structure which lets the rain sluice through. If you really
must start gardening when the soil is wet, then lay a builders'
plank on top of the soil and stand on top of that, which is why
a plank is in the Top 10 Most Essential pieces of gardening
equipment, but get your partner one for Christmas . . . Talk
about ungrateful.

Knowing what you've got
Clay
Before planting you need to know whether your soil is clay,
chalk or sand because different plants like different conditions. In extreme cases it's obvious. If the bare winter soil
looks like a scene out of World War I with great big sucking
puddles and you're squelching in a cold wet sponge, that's
clay. A bad case.

The difference between clay, chalk or sand is determined by porosity. In the case of clay the tiny clay particles are rammed tight together, often excluding air. Get your fingers in the wet soil and scoop out a gobby chunk and, no trouble, you can mould it into any shape you want. It's sticky goo. Plasticine. Make a hole in the ground and fill it with water and 30 minutes later the level hasn't changed. No drainage. And that same concrete compaction is there in summer. Try digging a pond and you'll practically need a pickaxe. And quite bizarrely, after a few days of baking heat, the top surface of a clay border shrinks and looks as if a mini earthquake has just struck with dry zigzagging cracks in the ground, often damaging the roots. Try getting weeds out and you'll need to hammer away at the ground with the tip of a trowel, chiselling them out of the ground. After 60 minutes you'll have a wrist like an exploding pumpkin.

The bad news is that clay takes yonks to warm up in spring. It stays cold and wet, and that means while your neighbour is sowing lettuces in early spring in his loose, crumbly, happy, fertile soil under his spanking new polytunnel you're waiting until early summer. The good news is that clay is potentially very fertile. What you've got to do is break it up – never when the ground is wet because the moment you've got your weight on it and squelch it down you just increase the problem – to improve the drainage and get more oxygen inside. And that means forking in huge quantities, depending on the severity, of horticultural grit, dry composted bark (not too much because it can reduce the nitrogen levels as it breaks down), leafmould and, best of all, mushroom compost because it contains gypsum, a natural clay breaker. Avoid adding wet and squishy compost because that'll increase the problem. If you're tempted to dig down to the poorer subsoil, either break it up or put a layer of the bark, leafmould and compost on top. But don't fork the subsoil up to the surface. Ever.

If you don't fight clay – and it is a constant fight, year after year, never stopping – you'll have to choose your plants very carefully, sticking to those that love this soil. Anything else will die in the cold, wet winter ground, rotting or drowning. Give plants a chance. Upgrade the clay. Make it crumbly.

Sand, chalk and dinosaurs

If not clay, what? The odds are that your soil is sandy or chalky, and you can easily test for sandy soil because it's incredibly gritty and sieves straight through splayed fingers. Pour water in a hole in the ground and it flushes through, taking the minerals and nutrients. The good news is that sandy soil warms up quickly in spring, though it cools quickly in winter, and can be improved by a regular feeding with great piles of organic matter. Because it holds onto water, these dollops also stop it drying out too quickly. Then add hefty mulches, like a cap on the soil, to keep the moisture locked in the ground.

Chalk is equally free draining, and you can spot it a mile away because it's skeleton white. If you've got chalk, are picking it up, holding it now, you're plugged directly into the past. This is chemically pure limestone from the time when the dinosaurs vanished.

Chalk is the Cretaceous past solidified, and is made of packed together trillions of miniscule fossils. Microscopic plankton skeletons which kept sinking to the sea bed, becoming lime mud and rock 80 million years ago. If you can find a geological map pinpointing the great stretches of chalk which still exist across the world, you'll see where the ancient chalk seas slapped across the continents millions of years ago, leaving these amazing deposits. Along the edges of the Weald and the white cliffs of Dover, on the facing French coast, into Denmark, even from the Black Sea into the Middle East, and from Texas to Mexico. (The whole of the British Isles was once covered in chalk, with the Weald, for example, a great big swollen dome; now only the outer northern and southern edges remain, the North and South Downs.) And here it is in your garden.

It certainly isn't fertile and throbbing with nutrients, so to grow the likes of roses you've got to dig a big planting hole, far wider and deeper than you need, and pack it with well-rotted compost and leafmould, and any bulky organic matter (but NOT mushroom compost, don't add that to chalk, that's bonkers, you'll just perpetuate the problem because there's invariably chalk packed in with the compost) to help keep moisture in the ground. The additions also help the soil hold onto the nutrients. Then add a slow-release organic feed, like blood, fish and bone.

If the bottom of the hole hits a solid layer of chalk, crack it open with a pickaxe, and year after year, after that, keep piling more manure onto the topsoil. Don't let up. The worms will keep dragging it down. And keep an eye on the plants in hot summers; the moment anything wilts give it an emergency drink. Quick. But there are plusses.

Chalky ground warms up quickly in spring, making it ideal for early bulbs, especially aconites and crocuses, and later tulips, and many plants do very well on just a few centimetres of thin soil over chalk, especially the likes of alder (*Alnus*), berberis, butterfly bush (*Buddleia davidii*), *Cotoneaster* 'Hybridus Pendulus', crown imperial (*Fritillaria imperialis*), hebe, Irish yew (*Taxus baccata*), the Judas tree (*Cercis siliquastrum*), *Juniperus communis*, lilac (*Syringa vulgaris*) and whitebeam (*Sorbus aria*). But don't even think about eucalyptus, poplars, spruces or willows. Birches are said to hate chalk, and they certainly don't thrive on it, but you'll often find them growing on it although they'll never get that big. Which might be, of course, just what you want in a small garden.

Digging-schmigging – who needs it?

If all this digging and soil improving sounds like hard work, it is. But you don't have to dig your garden. Think about it. No one goes around digging up the countryside, and the wildflowers grow perfectly well. So what are you doing? What happens if you stop?

You won't destroy your back, and you won't keep forking up buried weed seeds, exposing them to the light, creating extra work. Yes, you've got to keep improving the soil, but you just scatter on an autumn and spring mulch of organic matter and let the worms do the work, nuzzling it under ground. And you get more earthworms in a no-dig garden. If you want one thing, it's *earthworms*. They're churners, pulling organic matter down. They break it into fine particles and improve the drainage. In just 1 hectare (slightly bigger than Wembley's football pitch) of well-cared for ground they can create 10 million burrows, a chaotic air vent system. They oxygenate the soil. And according to Steve Jones' *Darwin's Island*, those worms, with everything else in the topsoil (the insects, spiders and snails, etc), make up 15 tons of flesh in that 1 hectare, which is tantamount to one and a half elephants shifting about under the ground, turning everything over. Or put another way, the number of individuals in one shovelful of top quality soil exceeds the number of people on the planet. (Be grateful you don't live in southern Australia where they've got the Giant Gippsland earthworm/*Megascolides australis* which can grow 3m/10ft long; it's just over 2.5cm/1in thick, with up to 500 body segments, and when that gets mad it squirts liquid 0.5m/20in in the air. Put your ear to the ground and you can even hear them escaping, sliming and slurping through tunnels when you thump the surface.) But back to the no-dig garden.

All this non-interference means that the healthy, open soil structure won't be disturbed, and that the organic matter in the topsoil stays exactly where it is. On top. The poorer subsoil stays underground. And, finally, the no-dig garden reduces the amount of watering because the moisture-retention is much better in the untouched top layers.

Ironically, you can't actually have a no-dig garden unless you've already got good soil, so you might have to dig for years before you can say "Never – Ever – Again". That's particularly true if you've got to improve the drainage, and eliminate heavy clay and/or perennial weeds.

But digging does have its good side. It's incredibly thera-
peutic and does give instant results. It aerates the soil, quickly
gets organic matter deep down, and tosses up pests, exposing
them to hungry predators.

Still not sure? Try no-digging in one bed and see what
happens. If you've got a raised bed though, you've probably
already been no-digging for years.

Who needs grass and soil? Try gravel

The ultimate no-dig garden is the gravel garden, but in case
you're thinking that means dumping tons of gravel on well-
worked, richly composted beds, that is NOT the idea. The
gravel isn't a glorified mulch, a grey background for traditional plants. You're basically recreating a Mediterranean-
type garden with rocky, stony, free-draining ground in a sunny
hotspot with less than say 63cm (25in) of rain a year.

The first big advantage is there's no staking, no feeding and
no mulching because you're going to grow plants which thrive
in these conditions. The alliums, bergenias, cistuses, ballotas,
lavenders, sea kale (*Crambe maritima*), *Tulipa sprengeri* and
grasses are Desperate Dans. They don't need mollycuddling.
That also means no lawn, no herbaceous borders and "No" to
the conventional language of gardening, the solid wodges of
hedge and barriers, and the framed openings into "garden
rooms". Gravel gardening is democratic and open plan, with
no hierarchies and no overpriced feature plants specially
imported from Italy.

The ultimate design has great sweeps of gravel over a wide
area, with paths meandering through island beds and plants
elbowing over the edges, rising in the middle in balls and
mounds and spires, letting the eye dart and ramble. If you love
the likes of huge verbascums with their long stretched grey
leaves and spurting stems barnacled with yellow flowers, the
packed-tight tiny flowers of the alliums making fat globes,
and stiff verticals of rich blue catmint (*Nepeta tuberosa*), go
for it.

The technical bit – the chemistry test

This tells you which kinds of plants to grow. It's not just a case of clay or chalk but acid or alkaline. Not brain-busting science. The quickest test is by looking at what your neighbours are growing. Heathers, pieris and rhododendrons, etc, spell acid ground, and if that's what you've got don't even think about growing alkaline-lovers, and vice-versa.

If you're unsure about the pH, get a cheap testing kit and take sample batches of soil from just beneath the surface. If you obviously have different kinds of soil around the garden, then take several samples from each separate area; mix them thoroughly, and use a small portion to give an average reading of that specific site. Or if there's just one kind of soil in the whole garden, again take samples from different areas and mix them up.

Even an eight-year-old can do it; just mix the soil sample with distilled water and a chemical in a test tube. Give it a shake, wait for the soil to settle and then check the colour of the water against a pH chart. This runs from 0–14, with a low reading indicating acid soil (that's low in lime and calcium), 7 being neutral, and 7.5 and higher indicating alkalinity (with plenty of lime and calcium, ideal for clematis, viburnums and lilac, etc). Most gardens are in the 6–8 zone. It takes 5 minutes. And if that's too fiddly, use an electronic meter.

Vegetables like slightly alkaline soil. If your soil is high in lime, it won't have much iron, so all your plants will put out sickly yellow leaves, but at least you'll know the solution. Pour a solution of chelated iron ("chelated" is just a technical term which means that the iron can easily be absorbed by the plants and does not end up as an insoluble sediment) around the roots; ie buy a packet of Sequestrene. It's also worth noting that some hydrangeas turn lilac-blue in acid soil, and pink in alkaline. That's certainly true of the *macrophylla* types, with only the white kind staying white. Now you can create blue flowers on alkaline soil, but you've got to use a special blueing compound with aluminium sulphate, and even then the results don't compete with the blue that you get when the plants are grown in acid. So forget it.

The soil's pH is rarely an insurmountable problem, provided you grow plants which love your conditions. Keep it simple. The only problem occurs when you want to grow an amazingly wonderful plant which doesn't like your soil's chemistry. With just one or two plants you're OK, but don't try changing the pH of your whole garden. It's easier to move house. You're far better off growing the likes of one or two azaleas in large barrels or a walled pit in the ground which you can fill with ericaceous (ie acid) compost. Easy peasy. You can also try using huge amounts of well-rotted sawdust, bracken, bark or pine needles to lower the pH, or sulphur chips for a quick fix, but you'll periodically have to keep adding more. It's not a one-off, permanent solution.

If the soil is too acid you can raise the pH reading by adding lime each and every autumn, but you'll have to do it in steps, with plenty of organic matter in winter followed by a helping of spring fertilizer. Don't try making an all-in-one cocktail to save time because it won't work. Lime plus the nitrogen in manure creates ammonia, and that can damage plants. But for 99.9 per cent of gardeners, all that's theory. With a pH of 6–8, which is what most people have, why worry?

Give plants the right diet

Now you know which kinds of plants you can grow, you might think about feeding them. (But if you've got the right plants in the right conditions, why bother?) Ideally plants get all their food from the ground. The roots spread out, like a matted web of mini drinking straws, sucking up moisture and nutrients which are held in the clay particles. That's why clay is a boon *and* a headache (being squelchy, hefty work in winter) while open, sandy, no-clay soil is a problem because any excess fertilizer gets washed straight through it. But what do plants need exactly?

The six key ingredients are, first, the big three – nitrogen

(N), phosphorus (P) and potassium (K) – followed by calcium, magnesium and sulphur, and others like boron and iron. Buy any box of fertilizer and it'll have an NPK reading on the back, for example 5:8:10, which immediately tells you that there are 5g of nitrogen per 100g of fertilizer, with 8g of phosphorus and 10g of potassium.

Nitrogen fuels leaf growth, phosphorus root growth and potassium gives extra flowers and fruit. If you want extra leaf growth for your lettuces use an N-high fertilizer, and for an extra batch of tomatoes use one high in K (especially because potassium can easily get leached out of the soil, making the levels in the garden low), but never overdose plants. It'd be like creating a test-tube creature with an enormous, smiley face and highly intelligent brain but miniscule arms and legs. Plants need good all-round, balanced growth, above and below ground, with good roots and strong stems.

If you're feeding permanent plants, not the annual vegetables for a bumper one-off crop, then you've got to restrict feeding to the first part of summer. The soft, sappy new growth needs time to toughen up before winter. Avoid sending the plant into overdrive late in the season, developing new growth which won't get time to harden off before the frosts. It'll get badly zapped.

So, the key question – when are plants nutrient-hungry? If they're not thriving, lack of nutrients *could be* the problem, but don't start unleashing a cocktail of chemicals because (a) they can do more harm than good especially (b) if the plants are floundering because of a completely different problem, and quite often that's a pest, disease, lack of water, or even poor soil structure which is stopping the roots from functioning properly. You need to investigate. But if more nutrients are the answer . . .

As a quick guide, poor spindly growth and yellowing lower leaves mean plants need a nitrogen fix; poor growth and sad yellow leaves point to extra phosphorus (though that's rarely a problem); and a really disappointing show with the leaf edges breaking out in yellow, purple or blue tints indicates plants need more potassium.

One good way of improving low nitrogen levels in the vegetable garden is by growing any legumes, that's peas and beans, and lupins and sweet peas (*Lathyrus odoratus*). They have this astonishing ability to increase the nitrogen in the soil, so make sure you keep moving the crops about from year to year (see rotation of crops, page 145), so that the legumes boost the nitrogen levels right across the site. Alternatively scatter pelleted poultry manure on the ground or apply dissolved sulphate of ammonia, while diluted Epsom salts are great at bolstering magnesium levels. And poor magnesium levels might be another cause of leaf-yellowing between the veins.

If you don't have a specific problem, then just stick to a good all-purpose feed every spring, unless you're the High Priest of Non-Intervention. You scatter the granular, inorganic kind (like Growmore) around the plants, or fork organic blood, fish and bone into the soil. Some plants, especially roses, benefit from a specific spring and midsummer feed geared at them, but if you've got any left over give it to the shrubs and they'll be just as grateful. Well-rotted manure and compost provide small, variable rates of feed (more a very light snack), depending on the source; they're best as soil improvers.

Battling extremes
Planting by the sea
The gales cause all the damage. Most books witter on about planting windbreaks to keep out the wind, but the odds are they'll get flattened by the first blast from France, Ostend or Flekkefjord. You've either got to work with what you've got, or call in an army of JCB diggers and lower parts of the garden, or erect artificial barriers to give the outer plants a chance to anchor their roots but, if you've got a monster prevailing wind . . .

Artificial barriers are the best bet for a gentler micro-climate, but when the wind hits a solid wall it flies up and thumps down, and you'll simply create separate areas of turbulence. You need filtering screens, picket fences or fencing mesh, halving the speed of the wind, but make sure they're nailed to stout posts set in concrete in the ground.

When planting shrubs to take over from or hide the screens (which are worth decorating with swags of thick rope or old fishermen's nets or lobster pots) don't make the mistake of buying large, substantial plants thinking that because they're more muscular they're better at getting a grip in the ground. Their roots won't get an immediate fix, and all that heavy top growth will go arse-up in the first gale. Buy young plants, provide a stake to keep them upright, and they'll quickly adapt and overtake larger plants which will take much, much longer to adapt. Top of the battering, salt-immune list are *Elaeagnus* x *ebbingei*, *Escallonia*, *Euonymus japonicus*, *Fatsia japonica*, *Griselinia littoralis*, *Pinus radiata*, *Pittosporum tobira*, the holm oak (*Quercus ilex*), phormiums, *Tamarix* and yuccas.

When planting, note that you'll have to keep an eye on new plants because the ground will be so free-draining they might need liquid aid, but don't create a regime of regular little drinks because all you'll do is encourage the roots to stay near the surface, waiting for the next slurp. You want them to bury down fast, getting good anchorage. After a good drink in spring add a thick mulch to keep the moisture locked in the ground and stop it quickly evaporating.

Next, the smaller plants. You need tough survivors, like *Santolina chamaecyparissus*, sea buckthorn (*Hippophae rhamnoides*), sea hollies (*Eryngium*, especially *E. agavifolium* and *E*. x *oliverianum*), sea lavender (*Limonium latifolium*) and sea pink (*Armeria maritima*), and come to that almost anything ending in *maritima* or *maritum*, such as *Mertensia* and *Silene*. In general try silver-leaved, hairy plants, hebes and olearias. Plants which wouldn't normally survive a seaside garden can be grown in the shelter of larger plants; trial and error. If you want fresh vegetables, then you've got to get a heavy-duty polytunnel, and the good news is that the mild climate, without frosts, should give terrific results, though you've got to make special beds with rich soil.

Best of all, the mild climate also means you can grow one of the most amazing plants in the world, *Echium pininana*. It comes from the Canaries, and puts on a power-spurt of growth in the first year, getting 1.5m (5ft) high, with extraordinary sprays of long, thin, jungly leaves and, if it survives that winter, you'll get a gigantic power-spike next year, to 3m (10ft) high, erupting in bluish flowers. And because it produces masses of seed, just one plant grown one year, and another the next, means you'll always have plenty of thickets.

Dry shade

Even if you've got one acre of damp shade you can dance round garden centres snapping up plants which like the gloom, but plants which like dry shade . . . Woa.

The first rule is try and improve the soil, and that means importing huge quantities of organic matter (especially leafmould) so that the soil has a better chance of retaining moisture. If the shade is cast by a giant evergreen tree then ferociously digging matter into the soil is going to damage the roots, so don't do it. Just lay the organic matter on the surface, lightly forking it in. It's not a total answer because the roots of the tree will still be sucking moisture out of the ground, and the canopy is going to act like a great big umbrella, deflecting the rain, but it helps. Then see if you can thin out the tree, letting in more light, first by "lifting the crown", which is the technical term for getting rid of the lower branches over winter, ie when the tree is dormant.

If you're doing the work yourself, stop and read this because you don't just saw through a branch. It'll be a *disaster*. As you saw down, the branch will give a great crack and rip, splinter and tear back, ripping into and damaging the main trunk. What you want is a smooth, sawn off surface. So . . .

Make a cut going up (Fig. 3), from under the branch, about 30cm (12in) *away* from the junction of branch and trunk,

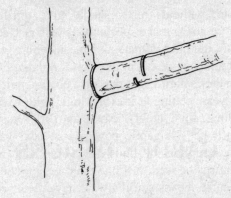

Fig. 3. How to cut a branch off a tree.

going through one-quarter of the branch. Then make a second cut, 2.5cm (1in) away, further along the branch, towards the tip, now cutting down. When the weight of the branch snaps down through the wood, it'll go straight back to the first cut, and can't tear further back into the trunk.

All you've then got to do is saw off this stump close to the trunk, but don't paint it over because it's a waste of money and time, and if anything you'll seal in infections. You can also thin the crown (getting rid of the top branches – hire professionals, don't do it yourself, this is dangerous work) but don't celebrate yet. This is not a permanent, one-off solution; all this pruning generates a great fuzz of new replacement growth, but it can easily be hacked off using secateurs or loppers.

Next step, the plants. Think about the winter-flowering *Mahonia aquifolium*, spring-flowering *Anemone nemorosa*, *Epimedium* x *rubrum*, *E.* x *versicolor* and *Brunnera macrophylla* 'Jack Frost', and the summer-flowering *Vinca major* and *minor*, with *Aucuba japonica* 'Variegata', *Coronilla valentina*, *Daphne laureola*, *Euphorbia amygdaloides* var. *robbiae*, x *Fatshedera lizei* and *Iris foetidissima*. The more light you can let in, and the moister the ground, the greater the range of plants. Problem solved.

2

GARDEN DESIGNS

Reliving the Renaissance
Before you tackle a new garden, fix the design. That's
the fun bit. Horticultural profiling. And what it says about
you.

Gardens with the strongest, punchiest geometric designs are
genetically bound to the Renaissance French/Italian look. And
they copied their gardens from classical antiquity, not real
gardens because they were then trashed in archaeological
fragments, but texts; vivid literary descriptions. Just Google
Versailles or Het Loo to see the mathematically manicured
lengths of hedge, the classical statues and focal points, the
parallel lines converging in the distance; the use of views,
avenues and recession. The pinpoint fascist mind ("You live,
You Die. Curve, Jump"). Which brings to mind Nabokov's
remark that "you can always count on a murderer for a fancy
prose style".

Such gardens don't photocopy the horticultural explosions
and flow and mad accidents of nature, they pack plants into
regular patterns – everything linked by the principles of
harmony and reason – and frame them; nothing out-of-place.
And one of the best ways of seeing such gardens isn't from
ground level – blag your way onto a press trip of the normally
private top floors of a stately home, where it's like looking
down on highly engineered Viennese pastries. An exponential,

exploding formula of fixed symbols: axes and topiary, cascades and fountains.

You'd have to be bonkers to do a kosher copy because that'd mean sticking to a staggeringly restricted number of plants. The sixteenth and seventeenth centuries *predated* the great plant hunters. No 'Chinese' Wilson and Francis Masson, David Douglas and George Forrest, Frank Kingdon-Ward and Robert Fortune. No daturas and red-hot pokers, bat plants and bananas. They might have been growing on Mars. Which is why when you walk around copies of early gardens the few plants are nicely spaced out, surrounded by bare earth, so that visitors could drool over what were often great rarities.

Formal gardens share the same pattern. The closer they are to the seat of power, the house or palace, the more ordered the look, and the more they replicate the architectural, well-proportioned hallmarks of the inside, copying, in Sir Roy Strong's words, the "three basic concepts: symmetry, perspective and pattern"; the further away you go, the closer you get to the "wild". Which was of course anything but wild, probably involving a *bosquet* or *boschetto*, a manicured small wood or formal planting of trees, sliced through by formal walks. And possibly even compartments with statues. All hail the dictating, explicable mind.

Late Renaissance gardens injected extra tricks and brio with organs powered by hydraulics, elaborate fountains and *giochi d'aqua*, or water games, with hidden water jets for scaring witless a visiting cardinal as he ambled down a path. Designers didn't stick to the same box of tricks, and in the baroque period became increasingly ambitious and more theatrical, using extra allegorical features, and even if you find all this completely OTT, the way in which they kept pushing back the boundaries of garden design is one rule which should be stamped on every gardener's forehead.

Cottage gardening
Cottage gardening is like jazz. You keep the pattern and break the rules. And you can forget about equal rights.

Real cottages were hell holes. Slums. And the everything-packed-in gardens doubled as a supermarket (with crops for humans and pigs, and herbs to jolly-up mealtime) and chemist (medicinal herbs), with a lively outburst of flowers. But because space was tight, everything was scrunched up. There wasn't room for a separate kitchen garden *and* spacious walks. The cottage garden was a pragmatic response to poverty. So who said otherwise?

Victorian artists like Helen Allingham. They created the romantic view of the cottage garden by painting chocolate box scenes, and they influenced gardening 'greats' like Gertrude Jekyll and then Margery Fish. The style caught on. It wasn't based on deprivation but required high taste and a smart eye. Also, the key element when using the likes of hollyhocks and old roses, poppies and sunflowers, and mallows and pinks, is to stick to natural materials. Use rustic wooden seats and arbours, with twigs for giving plants a leg up, and get rid of anything shiny and contemporary, especially aluminium. Give the plants free reign, merging, spreading and self-seeding, but nothing gets out of hand. Everything obeys. Plants aren't autonomous in charge of their own fate. This is an aesthetic with strict rules. And you're Pol Pot.

Think Mediterranean

The biggest lesson from Mediterranean gardens is think small, in COLOUR. The tiny courtyard gardens on the Greek islands and in Sicily, and the remote towns west of Seville, which no-one ever visits, show just how much colour you can pack into a small space, especially where there's a large white wall-canvas.

Grow trailing, tumbling, brightly coloured annuals and perennials, like pelargoniums and busy Lizzies, in small pots and hang them in rows on the wall, layering a vertical garden. Add to the fun by using anything that'll double as a container – old tin cans, boots, kettles, anything that'll last one season without disintegrating with wet compost packed inside, and which will take drainage holes fixed in the bottom. You'll need to make sure the containers are securely attached because wet compost doubles in weight, and if the plaster is disintegrating . . . Use chunky old woks at the base.

It helps to add a feature plant, such as an orange or lemon shrub (they're called trees but they don't get that tall, not in a container, and *not* in the UK), but if you don't have a Mediterranean climate then check if the plants are tender because if you leave them out all year they'll immediately get killed by the frost or rot with their roots in the cold, wet winter soil.

To highlight the look you could whitewash the walls, or paint them soft orange or even pale blue, but keep the design stylish, quiet and bare. Let the plants stand out. And remember you've got to do the watering, and if you don't use water-retaining gels that's a full-time job. The compost in small containers dries out incredibly quickly, so you've got to give them life-support every evening. Do it then and they'll get a long drink before the morning sun dries the moisture. The time-saving gels are added to the compost where they absorb water, swell up and gradually release it back for the plants to drink.

Copy the Japanese . . .

If you're short of design ideas, the Japanese look is packed with smart ideas. You don't have to go the whole way, and you don't have to know the rules. And there's no one fixed, typical Japanese garden but there are key themes.

The first thing Japanese gardens did was to attract divine spirits. To confuse and repel anything evil they used every-whichway paths, and odd numbers of plants and stones (a) to add a dash of wildness and (b) because the even numbers were very unlucky.

The early Shinto religion (more concerned with life down-here than up-there) believed that divine spirits (*kami*) inhabited natural phenomena – rocks and stones, mountains and trees – and that's why stones are not the add-on, bung-in items in Western gardens. They have a rich, spiritual life. They add purity and antiquity, evoking anything from a mountain, stream, waterfall or leaping fish to an image from an ancient text. Each stone is hand picked and precisely placed. And one large, extraordinary stone might be enough for one garden provided it throbs with *gravitas*. The cost of old, uncut stones in subdued colours and/or when covered with moss were outrageous.

Abstract dry gardens became increasingly popular thanks to the Buddhist Zen monks who created them because they needed contemplative retreats, apparently to escape the civil war. The gardens were a kind of horticultural version of yoga, calming and transporting, wafting the essence of a quiet, still universe out of an open, artful area filled with dry gravel (invariably signifying the sea) and stones (mountains). They were created to perpetuate and elide layers of meaning. You experience the unity underlying everything (a kind of spiritual string theory), and stretch out to become part of the universe. The key ingredients were metamorphic rock, stones, paths, gravel and granitic sand.

Stepping stones and paths were used to guarantee that visitors approached the main garden or tea house ceremony (a late twelfth-century Chinese import, though 'embellished hut' might be more apposite) in the right, refined spirit. They didn't want anyone sploshing through mud and pounding across the carefully cultivated moss on their way to such a purifying, peaceful ritual.

Other key ingredients include bamboo fencing and stone ornaments – towers, buddhas, herons and cranes, lanterns and bridges, and especially the clack-clacking of a *shishi odoshi* (or deer scarer) used by farmers, with water repeatedly pouring into a bamboo pipe which, when empty, flips back and whacks against a rock. Also use shallow ponds and streams, with flashing dazzling carp to contrast with the stillness.

When trying a Japanese garden, the key point is to ignore the traditional Western obsession with symmetry and perspective and focal points, and a great green central lawn. Their gardens unfold, gradually, giving a multiplicity of views past highly stylized plants. Use pruned, trained pines to give instant antiquity and a see-through, wizzened effect. Look for the inherent shape of a tree or shrub, and strip away everything else to reveal its essence. If a young pine has a clutter of branches, saw off anything which detracts from its basic shape, aim to create views through it, and contort the growing trunk into, say, a forward-slanting S-bend using weights or string and pegs stuck in the ground to angle the branches until they permanently assume that shape. Also try cherries for a pillow-bang of blossom, called *sakura*, using the likes of the pink *Prunus* 'Kanzan' and white 'Shirofugen', the Japanese maple (*Acer japonicum)* and cypress (*Cupressus*), black pines (*Pinus thunbergii*), paulownias and magnolias. The dominant note is green. Not monotonous green but lime green, olive, apple…

Guarantee strong, year-round uniformity (the gardens don't go phutt and collapse like Western borders when they're mugged by frost), the elegant use of space, asymmetry and gentle movement, and approach everything with a surgeon's eye. And with luck you'll have a Japanese garden.

Or the Chinese

If Japanese gardens are goody two-shoes, all rarified austerity, Chinese gardens are like Chaucer's monks, burping, belching and godly.

Their gardeners liked real water, not symbols. They didn't remorselessly regulate nature. They created areas where people could live, argue and play. The designers didn't subsume everything to a set of abstract principles, they personalized their gardens. Classical designs were like a great cosmic stir fry with everything thrown in, and just as Chinese science was not divorced from ethics (which happened in the

West, with the rise of modern science in the seventeenth century), so there was no discrimination between different forms of experience. The Chinese had an organic, holistic theory of the universe. Everything was included, the natural and supernatural, church and state, the past, present, and future, private and public. The frivolous co-existed with philosophy, the mundane and the fabulous. And you can see all this in their gardens.

Classic Chinese gardens weren't lavishly planted like Western ones, they were *built*, and in the seventeenth-century gardening manual *Yuan Ye* plants hardly get a look in. Gardeners were almost architects. The prime ingredients were buildings and stone, water and trees, with flowers playing a minor but larger part than in Japanese designs. And the energies keeping everything in balance were the *yin* and *yang*. The *yin* is the soft, feminine, inward, gathering element (eg water) and the *yang* the masculine – the outward and bursting, upright and bony (eg stone). And in one spectacular act of literalism, an ancient emperor lowered the levels of dangerous floodwaters by packing off 200 wagons loaded with "super-fluous [*yin*] women". And yes, it did work. The levels went down. They *did*.

The rocks used in Chinese gardens are more suggestive and showier than the quieter, introvert Japanese kind. The biggest Chinese garden rock might be 15m (50ft) high. And the wider the range of shapes, the better. Ideally some were placed to emerge out of the morning mist, magnifying their sense of mystery. Rocks gave a glimpse into other worlds, naturalistic and spiritual, and reading them is quite a skill. Optical illusions were also vital. Short streams could be made to look like long ones, curling off into the distance; they'd start wide, get thinner, and disappear behind rocks where they'd promptly end.

But how were these great classical gardens constructed? Typically, with a series of open-roofed courtyards, cobbled or paved, often inlaid with mosaics. White walls silhouette features (a rock or small, spare angular tree). There are subtle, painterly compositions within each space with a main subject (like a pomegranate tree), and scenes glimpsed through an intricate filigreed or imaginatively shaped window (say resembling a flower or leaf), into the next yard. So a small overall area becomes large as you amble this way and that, on and on, from scene to scene. Sun and shade, large and small, *yin* and *yang*. From Confucian order to the open garden, and to the importance of our place in nature.

The Chinese concentrated on their traditional favourite plants, sticking to paulownias, fruit trees (eg bananas), pines, thuja, the pagoda tree (*Sophora japonica*), and plants with medicinal, moral, magical and aesthetic properties. Ancient twisted trees were in; the rare hardly counted. They were, and still are, grown with a greater degree of isolation than in Western gardens where bare earth and gaps are a sin. The Chinese liked to isolate their forms and scents, often against a bare wall or in pots, a way of highlighting seasonal change.

Classical Chinese gardens can't be interpreted in Western terms with their in-your-face immediate needs, but in terms of Oriental gods and landscape painting, literature and nature, and Buddhism's view of the universe, and that most certainly doesn't involve an empty geographical (Western) space, sitting there waiting to be colonized. Their gardens were far more complex and other-worldly than anything made in the West.

Cloud pruning

If Chinese and Japanese designs sound like lofty, unrealizable gobbledegook, cloud pruning isn't. Japanese cloud-pruned shrubs (Fig. 4) make amazing (fantastically expensive, but we'll come to that) features, and if you've never seen one before, this is what you get. A shrub with say five or six branches, each of which is bare right to the end when it explodes in a wonky ball of green, like gigantic Brussel sprouts. Japanese holly (*Ilex crenata*) is the traditional choice for one very good reason, the

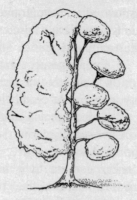

Fig. 4. Cloud pruning.

packed-tight-together dark green leaves are very small and they can easily be trimmed without the problems associated with slashing through, and without disfiguring, larger leaves. Also try Chinese privet (*Ligustrum delavayanum*).

You can easily grow one yourself, but don't make the mistake of stripping off all the leaves from a young plant because you want it to grow quickly, and the best way of getting the branches to thicken and develop is by leaving on its food-making factory (the foliage). Once the plant is the right height, then attack. Remove all the unnecessary growth. "What's unnecessary?" Ah! The hard part; you've got to envisage its "essential", hidden, X-ray-like shape, and then strip away everything to leave just that: several shapely branches with a batch of leaves at the end, and then start snipping that into topiarized balls. If it's being grown in a pot make sure the compost gets regularly watered, and feed with blood, fish and bone. Old, shapely cloud-pruned specimens can cost thousands. Cuttings are free.

Inject Islamic patterns
If you're lucky enough to have a large, baking, south-facing courtyard, and you've had it with traditional Western straight lines, try a snapshot from an Islamic garden. A long shallow

pool or rill running down the centre, framed by elegant shady shapes. Paradise *à la* Koran. Early Islamic designs were based on the *chahar bagh*, meaning garden divided into four, where the blessed would lie among pomegranate trees and voluptuous fountains. But if you're going to create this kind of oasis you've got to ditch your ego. Big egos belong with Italians in the Renaissance, when theatrical water displays became increasingly OTT, involving staggering sums of money and wilder rounds of applause.

In time Islamic designs became more elaborate, and anyone who has been to the Real Alcazar palace in Seville and seen the patterning on the walls understands immediately how they saw things. No hierarchical Christian groupings of sinners, disciples and angels, fixed around the Holy Triumverate. Islamic art replicates the infinite universe, with whole walls and domed ceilings snaking and spinning never-ending intricate, complex, bewildering patterns. Without beginning, without end. Which was how they designed many gardens. Spiralling around and away. Which was also in complete contrast to eighteenth-century, landscape, aristocratic Western gardens, the kind that whisk you on a self-congratulatory garden tour, setting out a historical narrative using major props like whacking great big classical statues and temples and views, confirming your, yes *your* (very important) place in the scheme of things. Islamic gardens don't do that. They expose the elegance within the godly.

Contemporary gardens
Right. Forget about Victorian gardens; everything overseas; about William Morris and the pre-Raphaelites, and the Arts and Crafts gardens brandished by Edwin Lutyens and Gertrude Jekyll, and wonky, eclectic Sissinghurst. Or perhaps not. Sissinghurst is like a beautiful throbbing boil on the bum. You can't stop having a look.

It's totally British. An aristo-lesbian writer and a gay MP; small, unpredictably arranged pockets of garden packed with old roses; a restored Elizabethan idyll of a (it must have been *freezing* in winter) castle; lashings of posh hanky-panky; and can-do amateurs thrashing professional designers. (Think about the most striking recent UK gardens and most were made by amateurs. Amateurs – except for Derek Jarman – with a very decent chunk of land, though you could argue his garden had more "borrowed" land that the lot of them, being slap in the middle of the Dungenness coast. And – this is the point – not one has or had a garden design diploma hanging in the loo. Not Charles Jencks, Beth Chatto, Christopher Lloyd, Rosemary Verey, Sir Roy Strong, Jarman or Ian Hamilton Finlay, etc.) But back to Sissinghurst. It had a strongly struc-tured, sub-sub-sub Italianate, intimate, highly idiosyncratic (at times nearly bonkers) design and lavish planting. Anyone can do it, that was the message. And most tried. Are *still* trying. But if you want to be up-to-date . . .

Try Modernism, which more or less means anything post-1920, invariably with a functional, architectural (ie tediously geometrically predictable) link between house and garden (read anything by John Brookes), Minimalism (a razor blade away from sensory deprivation and a 1930s look) or, what you really need, a Conceptual garden. A garden with a cracking idea which underpins every element. The idea is paramount. The design focuses on the intellectual process; plants come second. Hence, Charles Jencks' (and his late wife's) Garden of Cosmic Speculation in Scotland (30 acres at the last count).

It's a horticultural interpretation/exploration/metaphorical representation of cosmology. It doesn't matter if you're a complete thicko about DNA and the double helix, waveforms, solitons, radio waves and brain waves, particles and fractals, how it began and where it'll end, what counts is the highly unexpected, curvy, surreal beauty of twisting, spiralling metal sculptures and tear-drop lakes hemmed in by steeply rising, sculptured, terraced sides inspired by scientific imaginings, diagrams and theory. Dahlias don't get a look in. What counts is the upbeat, prepotent use of unlikely shapes and patterns.

Using the latest scientific (or non-traditional gardening) imagery means new ways of being inventive.

Ivan Hicks's Garden In Mind (a walled garden in Hampshire, long since disgracefully bulldozed) was a Surrealist's playpen. It bristled with absurdly ignored ideas. The garden was packed with discarded metal odds and sods as sculptures, with saplings bent into spiders' webs and bridges and wigwams, and trees trained into wonky shapes. He once told me he loved nipping down to B&Q to see what he could stick in a flowerbed. Hicks would nip the top off a vertical tree stem when it was, say, 1.2m (4ft) high and train the top two new replacement shoots around a large circle, fixed in place, and eventually remove this metal template, leaving a sturdy mid-air circular picture frame hovering on one leg. And this whacky, startling, new (to most people) way of seeing shapes is what keeps gardening alive.

Other designers worth Googling include Jacques Wirtz, Roberto Burle Marx and Topher Delaney.

Wildlife gardens and drifts

Which brings us to wildlife gardens. This means giving trees – galaxies of biodiversity – space to grow, and creating large communal gardens where managed areas can be left for the wildlife. Grow tough, no-nonsense native plants giving them room to spread; don't worry about paltry weeds. A weed is only a prejudice. An obstinate anything growing exactly where it shouldn't. But marauding invaders – they need to be nuked to give others a chance. All of which means that the local, native plants – which will be happy in your conditions – won't need pampering. No special watering, deadheading or prettifying. Wildlife gardening means acquiring a new, non-prissy set of aesthetics.

What you don't want though is Japanese knotweed (*Fallopia japonica*). It spurts out beautiful pale green stems with vertical maroon dashes (I'm looking at one as I write; I just picked it by the pond) and makes a great leafy grove thumping 2.1m (7ft) high each summer. You can see why it was imported in 1825. But it's an indestructible, overpowering juggernaut, and if you're mad enough to encourage it in the wild they'll 'ave you. It's breaking the law. I tried killing my clump by cutting off the stems low down and pouring bleach down the central tube but they just belched, stretched and shot up again. Keep cutting back the new stems and it won't erupt but it's flexing its muscles underground and, in bad cases, you'll need to call in the professionals to squirt it with agent orange or whatever they use. Or check out *www.rhs.org.uk/advice/profiles0604/japanese_knotweed.asp*.

If you've got a massive garden, stick to meandering drifts of native perennials (they recently became incredibly trendy) which die down in winter, and grasses, which don't need cutting back until late winter, leaving features through the splatter and mud, but you must cut back before spring or you'll massacre the new shoots. The garden is meant to resemble a healthy, free-flowing slab of countryside which begs the question, why are you copying *that*? How can you possibly *compete*? Can't you be engagingly wittier? However it is low maintenance because you're choosing plants which thrive in your conditions so you can forget about pumping them up with chemicals to create Olympic-size plants. This also means you don't need a JCB to reshape the wonky topography; if you've got banks, bumps and slopes, so what? And if you're a fan of designer James van Sweden, forget about a lawn. Go for unpredictably angled paths between the plants and a patch of rough ground for a deckchair.

If you need more than great long lines of lavender and miscanthus, Google Sticky Wicket garden and copy Pam Lewis's idea for narrowish circular beds, one within the other, packed with nectar plants, kept separate by circular paths. Horticultural aposiopesis. A good variation involves two long, wide borders up either side of the garden with paths and/or streams meandering within them, so that you can wander and sit in your border. Borders don't have to exclude.

Get the planting right, and the wildlife should move in. You'll then have a balanced ecosystem with plenty of killers to eliminate the pests attacking your plants. The commonest killer is the common flower bug which spends the winters resting under the bark and the summers picnicking on aphids and spider mites. The rove beetles – and there are just under 1,000 species in the UK – devour fungi, decaying plant matter and slugs, while spotted ladybirds (and the UK has 46 different species) take aphids and plant lice, with one seven-spot ladybird being capable of munching through 5,000 aphids per annum.

The only problem is that ordinary ladybirds are now being eaten by the bigger, greedier Harlequin kind, which originally came from Asia. They were meant to eliminate European pests but in so doing have become a helluva pest, and now bivouac in southeast England. They're hard to identify immediately because they can have from 0–21 orange-red or black spots, though most in the UK have 15–21, but they will be 5mm (⅕in) or more long. They usually live on deciduous trees and patches of nettle, and when they are not attacking our native ladybirds they're eating all their food.

Other friendly predators include wasps (with a liking for caterpillars and aphids), and, with climate change accelerating, it's just a matter of decades before Kent is packed with praying mantises, the spiny front legs spearing a goldfinch in the chest, teeth ripping the neck, munching it alive. (That's how they dine.) And of course all these predators are being eaten by everything else. Oh to hear their screams. To have them amplified through speakers in the trees. But the good news is when you see rose buds packed with aphids, you can let the wildlife tackle the problem. Why spray?

3

THE STRUCTURAL BASICS

Walls

How you define the edge of your garden is between you and (a) your psychiatrist and (b) bank manager. If your garden is a great "Keep Out" V sign, being a *hortus conclusus* (which is actually a garden within a garden, an enclosed space, like the Virgin Mary's intact virginity) then hedges and walls do the job. Sunny high walls double as fantastic radiators because they soak up the heat and bounce it back, which is why every last inch should be covered with pears and figs, especially the tender kind, so they'll fatten; plopping and juicy. Walls also block gales, but note that the wind will fly up, over and down, meaning yes you get shelter but you can't get rid of its thumping, flattening down-bash. You simply give it another target. But a smallish garden with a high, wrap-around wall creates a much warmer, sleepier microclimate.

The choice of materials is huge, and in the case of stone and brick, expensive, so no to Bob The Builder up the road. Also forget panel fences because even treated wood periodically rots and needs replacing. Get a garden designer (and always check their CV, make them BEG for work) who knows the options. Try . . .

• Gabions (stone packed into long, thin, rectangular metal

cages) which is very fashionable/staggeringly ugly (it's your call, but, come on, do you really want them?).

• A dry-stone wall with plants in the gaps.

• Simple (sinuous, curvy) rendered blockwork with a pastel wash.

• A sturdy wall with Oriental openings, ie a large round hole, called a moon gate, for stepping through into another garden, or peephole windows giving a view of a spectacular plant.

• A sturdy wall with a real old window frame.

• Stone slabs bolted to a concrete wall.

• Concrete patterned with seashells, pottery or messages.

• Walls with inset mirrors or gaps for stained-glass windows.

• Flat surfaces for light shows after dark.

• And walls made of glass and metal.

As with wine, quality = price. For the best walls, marry a Hedge Fund manager from South America.

Hedges
Hedges filter strong winds, and the stronger the wind, the thicker you want that hedge. Go for a fat, chunky large-leaved evergreen, but if you intend cutting back go for a small-leaved alternative like box because the large ones look shocking when slashed and disfigured.

Good hedge contenders include any solid wodge of bamboo, *Elaeagnus* x *ebbingei* (and cultivars with flashy, variegated leaves), *Euonymus japonicus*, *Garrya elliptica*, *Griselinia littoralis*, holly (*Ilex*), *Olearia traversii*, *Podocarpus nivalis* and *P. salignus,* and Portugal laurel (*Prunus lusitanica*). Dark greens, such as yew (*Taxus baccata*), make the best backdrop for the likes of white tulips. Check to see if box has been zapped in your area because box blight can massacre a hedge; if growing one, give an annual spring feed of seaweed fertilizer to keep it fighting fit, and trim twice a year, in spring and late summer. And box is a good choice for shade. Don't be snobbish thinking everyone grows a privet; they grow it because it's very effective. Ditto conifers, which give fantastic protection for over-wintering birds.

If you need a hedge like barbed wire, the Chinese *Berberis julianae* is death by a thousand cuts. It's rigid with vicious spines, each 5cm (2in) long. They're grouped in threes, and stab out just below each shiny leaf (and *even they've* got sharp teeth around the edges) so you get the triplets poking out every 5cm (2in) up the stem. One spine points to the left, one to the right, and one straight between. Get through that. My RHS plant encyclopedia says it grows 3m (10ft) high (Whatttt!); mine is double that and *still* growing. My tree surgeon had to get into a medieval diving suit and that was before he looked at it. "Slice off 4ft," I said, "and get on with it". The whole thing blowtorches autumn orange-red and splatters yellow flowers in spring. Then millions of bees land.

If you're growing smooth walls of evergreen hedge, don't miss a trick. Shape the tops in peaking then descending waves – curving up-down, up and down; or keep it flat and then leave regularly spaced out shoots to be topiarized into turrets, balls or cubes; cut out exits and doorways (inserting a real door from a skip), and hollowed-out insets for a chair; or simply let the whole thing splurge belly out then curve in, like stacked, packed together stomachs (flabby, held-in and misshapen). A hedge is topiary waiting to happen.

Informal hedges (good for wildlife) are much less effort,

and are easily grown with native trees and shrubs, but note that everything here is deciduous, apart from the holly, so in winter you'll get a fuzzy filtering screen. Failsafe ingredients include blackthorn (*Prunus spinosa*) – with clustering, round, shiny blackish 'grapes', initially with a powdery covering, for making sloe gin – crab apple (*Malus sylvestris*), field maple (*Acer campestre*), guelder rose (*Viburnum opulus*), hawthorn (*Crataegus monogyna*), hazel (*Corylus*), spindle (*Euonymus europaeus*) and an evergreen holly (go for the self-pollinating evergreen *Ilex aquifolium* 'J.C. van Tol' and you won't have to grow a male and female to get the berries). Then add an old man's beard (*Clematis vitalba*) and it'll climb, scramble and leg it with gobbets of tufty seedheads.

If using conifers, prune them at least twice a year to keep them in shape. If they turn into big-bellied slobs they're impossible to cut back too hard because the old wood won't regenerate. You're left with a brown gap. An eyesore. With a bad case, chuck it out and start again.

Leyland cypress – who's to blame?
Bull-brained oafs. The leylandii is a throbbing great big rocket of a conifer, all flat sprays of dark green leaves tapering to a point about 35m (120ft) up there, so growing a Berlin Wall is a flaming, appalling outrage to those on the other side. But you can . . .

Keep it short with judicious pruning. In its first spring nip back any long sideshoots and give a follow-up shearing up the sides in midsummer, and continue keeping the sides nicely shaved back in following years, but don't cut right back into old wood because it won't reshoot. (That's a tip if you live on the other side.) When it's close to the required height, cut back the tops, and thereafter keep giving it trims during the growing season. Never trim in autumn because the shoots start dying back from the tip. If you have got one which is already too tall, just cut back the top by about one-third in spring, but if it ends up very short, wide and bonkers chuck it on the bonfire. Which you might well need to do if it gets attacked by the killer Cypress aphid. Botanists still aren't quite sure how they kill – either by injecting poison or by stopping water being piped through the plant.

Before messing with x *Cupressocyparis leylandii* it's worth (1) checking whether there are any problems with dieback in your area and (2) knowing what you're dealing with. It has got the genes of two American giants, the 30m (100ft) high *Chamaecyparis nootkatensis* and the even taller *Cupressus macrocarpa*, and their leylandii sprogget was bizarrely found growing in Wales in the late 1880s. It zooms up about 1m (3½ft) a year for 20 years or so before putting on the brakes and growing at a still pretty fast 60cm (2ft) a year. Look after it and you'll get a quick-growing windbreak-cum-hedge. Cultivars (contact a specialist nursery) come in green tinged with grey, bluish-grey, bronze, yellow and cream. Take your pick. Unless you want a . . .

Bamboo (for screens and hedges)

- Bamboo can grow 90cm (3ft) a day at full throttle and makes thick, dense, impenetrable screens.

- Bamboos are high-octane growers from early to late summer. Measure the new growth once a week and you'll see what I mean. Canes reach their full height in one season.

- The oldest canes in a clump are the thinnest and shortest. The new ones are increasingly thicker and taller.

- And the leaves and branches on the newest canes appear increasingly higher up. By the time the canes are 2.5cm (1in) thick the first leaves can be over head high.

- You can thin out clumps to give a filtered view to other parts of the garden, or thin them out and tie up the tops to create an instant igloo.

- Bamboos are easily grown, greedy and thirsty. Give them a spring mulch of compost so they don't dry out, with a mid-summer sprinkling of Growmore, and add grit to the soil for good drainage. For a wind- and drought-tolerant bamboo that'll grow where others won't, try *Thamnocalamus tessellatus*, with flashy white sheaths over the new canes.

- Their anchoring rootballs don't go deep, invariably about 23cm (9in) down, which means that if young plants put on plenty of topgrowth and are growing in a windy, open site they're likely to get upended in a gale until securely anchored and rooted.

- If putting in underground barriers to restrict their spread, dig down at least 50cm (20in).

- And never grow bamboo near a pond unless you want the canes spearing up through the liner, puncturing it.

Basically, there are three kinds of bamboo. First, those with tall, thickish canes, 4m (12ft) high and over, possibly hitting 6m (20ft). *Phyllostachys* has the best colours. For orange-yellow canes with green vertical stripes get *P. aureosulcata* 'Spectabilis'. Its minimum ground space is about 90sq cm (3sq ft). *P. a.* 'Aureocaulis' is a better yellow but hasn't got the stripes. The bright orange-yellow, moderately invasive *P. bambusoides* 'Holochrysa' has an occasional stripe, while *P. vivax* 'Aureocaulis' is one of the best of the yellows with striking random green stripes and panels. All look best when lit by the winter sun, and be prepared to keep barging in to snip off the leafy growth so that the canes are clearly visible. New canes keep jabbing up through the soil but if they get out of hand, slice them off with a spade.

The second group, and one of the best for hedges, is *Fargesia*, not least because it stays under a very manageable 5m (15ft) high. The dark purple *F. nitida* is happy in shade, while the new *F. n.* 'Jiuzhaigou' develops reddish canes. The rough, tough *F. robusta* gets slightly taller than its relatives, and makes a burst of rich green leaves.

The third kind, but never for hedges, makes seriously invasive groundcover. There's the 90cm (3ft) high *Sasa veitchii*, and 30cm (1ft) high *Pleioblastus pygmaeus*, and yes you can even mow it. They'll eventually cover one acre.

Paths

Paths are the most crucial part of the garden. Borders? Easy. Hedges? Peasy. But paths.

First, forget about getting from A to B. Paths are for getting you there *in style*. And that means keeping the eye moving around, down and up, especially if you vary the style of the path as it moves around the garden. Use irregular stepping stones interspersed with spring tulips, summer daisies and all-year-round thymes and/or moss. The more you space out the irregular stones the more you force people to look down and that slows their pace. That's a good trick if you're bringing them to a view where they're meant to stop and reinforces the message that they're being sent to a different part of the garden.

When leading to a formal set-view, use formal patterns: so use frost-proof (if you don't check they are, you're burning your money) bricks in a herringbone; or paving slabs edged by cobbles; or paving slabs with a rill running down the middle; or coloured ceramic tiles well spaced out in a brick path, with the tiles getting closer together as you want people to pick up speed and move on. Wide paths can be broken up with large inset mosaics/symbols made from the likes of pebbles, discs, shells, coloured glass, etc, set in concrete.

The last thing you want with a long straight garden is one long straight path. A garden, no matter how small, has to be explored and fingered and relished. Don't expose everything in one go. Use lengths of path taking you on different journeys. Paths snaking away and disappearing behind a distant bush suggest that the garden goes on and on, and if they are wider in the foreground and narrower in the distance, you might even hint that the garden is very long. That's equally true if the path takes people the long way around. Confuse visitors. Well that's the theory. The reality means making sure that the path is (a) wide and strong enough for a wheelbarrow and (b) ideally for two people walking side by side, while checking that (c) it doesn't pass under the shade of a tree or it'll get covered by wet winter slime (and that especially applies to decking) and (d) that heavy rain quickly drains away.

Before buying any material, take home a sampler to see if the look works in bright sun and rain, and because new materials change colour once weathered. A good alternative is buying from an architectural salvage yard, or anywhere selling old paving stones, slate and roof tiles.

The easiest path is made of gravel, but even that takes a bit of work. You've got to excavate the proposed path so that it's 10cm (4in) deep, and frame the edges with wooden boards fixed in place. Cover the base with scalpings from a builders' yard and then slam them down using a compressing machine, giving a hard, compact surface. Then the gravel goes on top. If you don't do this you'll keep pressing the gravel down into the soil and (expensively) have to keep topping it up.

Once you've played around with ideas get hold of an expert because laying complex, arty, elaborate, intricate paths takes gallons of know-how. And time.

Silver birch and hazel structures

Use old boat masts, oars, twisty lengths of painted scrap metal, etc, for fun uprights and arches. Top them with anything from spangly disco balls to cones.

If you need rustic wigwam supports for the likes of quick-sprinting sweet peas and nasturtiums, use about eight head-high lengths of silver birch and make sure that each is firmly planted in the ground (stamp hard on the soil), in a circle, with their heads bound tight together at the top. They'll need locking together to give extra stability, and that means weaving and binding the clustered side growth together, which also provides the horizontal rungs for the climbers to grab onto. And weed the whole area thoroughly before you start, getting out every last scrap of root.

Tunnels can be made from bendy, flexible, live lengths of hazel (*Corylus avellana*), and they need to be planted about 30cm (1ft) apart and 25cm (10in) in the ground, opposite each other. Bind and tie them together where they meet in the middle, and new shoots from the base will provide extra arching-over growth which needs to be woven and tied around the initial arch, providing extra support. Side branches can be trained up the length of the tunnel. If any new growth starts soaring upwards, cut it right back to keep the shape of the tunnel. Keep the planting area weed-free.

Willow structures and edging

Plant a coppiced willow rod (*Salix viminalis*) in damp ground and it'll quickly root and grow. Don't believe it? That's how crack willow (*Salix fragilis*) self-propagates. Bits of twig snap and go flying in a gale and land in damp ground and bingo, a new tree. That fertility makes willow the most prolific natural fencing.

Once each rod is fixed in moist ground it'll quickly root and easily grow 3.7m (12ft) a year. Use it to grow giant caves and, for a fence (Fig. 5), lengths of willow (available on scores of websites) planted in a well-weeded row, 25cm (10in) deep and one pace apart. They'll need some support to keep them in position, so hammer stout posts into the ground and join them with lengths of nailed-up taut wire. Weave the willow rods in a criss-crossing upward angle of 45 degrees between the wires, and cut off the tops at 1.4m (4½ft) high. Also try tepees, arbours, igloos and sin bins.

Woven, horizontal lengths of willow also make excellent ankle-high edging for flower beds. Weave the rods around

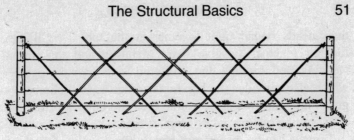

Fig. 5. Willow structures.

short vertical pegs hammered into the ground, leaving about 20–25cm (8–10in) above ground.

When edging areas of lawn with metal strips, bricks or a wooden plank on its edge make sure that the barrier separating the lawn from the path or flower bed is flush with the grass or you won't be able to mow right up to the edge. The path or soil should be at a slightly lower level.

4

TREES

What's inside a tree?

It's worth knowing what happens in a tree and how it grows. Trees stand up bone hard and don't flop because of a chemical called lignin, without which they'd go kaput, and because they are packed with zillions of miniscule hollow tubes rammed tight together. They reinforce the whole. The bark is like a waterproof suit of shock-absorbing armour and protects the insides and helps regulate the temperature. Peel that back and you'll find the thin width of the phloem, the prime feeding channel that's full of sap and sugar. Then comes the pale beige sapwood, the drinking channel through which water gets sucked up from the top. We're not talking dribs and drabs but up to 500 litres (110 gallons) a day in extreme cases. And the brown centre is the dead heartwood which also helps keep this massive structure upright.

Trees grow up from the top (which means all the branches stay at the same height *forever*), and simultaneously expand inside, beneath the bark. This creates the visible growth rings, and the gaps between each ring will differ because the amount of annual growth will differ, depending on the weather.

The leaves (and mature trees might have five million) constitute a giant photosynthetic, oxygen-producing factory. Yes, the deciduous trees lose their leaves in autumn, but does an evergreen hang onto its leaves forever? No. It also sheds them, big time, and gains new ones in spring. Holly (*Ilex*) holds onto its leaves for three years before they drop.

Quiz time
- The world's tallest tree? A coastal redwood (*Sequoia sempervirens*) at 115.5m (378.9ft).

- The oldest? A Bristlecone pine (*Pinus longaeva*) at 4,600 years.

- The widest trunk? A distorted Montezuma bald cypress (*Taxodium mucronatum*), a pigeon's bum short of 11.5m (38ft).

- And the most extensive, thanks to its prolific suckers (ie shoots growing up from the roots)? An aspen (*Populus tremuloides*); it has expanded and multiplied to generate a wood exceeding 100 acres. All that from one plant.

Is biggest best?

No. The only excuse for buying a large tree is when you need an instant (expensive) effect. Otherwise, choose a small, healthy, 90cm (3ft) high tree with an excellent root system, and the importance of the latter is staggering. You wouldn't buy a Bentley with a rubbish engine. Why do that with a plant?

When tall trees are loaded up and driven from a nursery to your garden, they suffer a huge shock. Out of the pot, with no more shelter, into the open ground and probably an exposed site. The tall stagnate and do not race away, while the (cheaper) young trees recover much more quickly and eventually overtake them.

Trees being raised out in the open are sold while dormant, without any soil around the roots (called bare root). The act of digging them up damages the roots, and again small trees recover much more quickly.

Is there a right way to plant a tree?

Yes, and that principally means ignoring everything you read
in old books. The traditional idea was to pamper them by
digging a highly nutritious hole full of the finest compost
giving a high-octane diet, but the latest advice is do that and
you'll kill it.

If growing just a few native trees, you can slam your spade
in the ground, lever it back creating a V shape (Fig. 6), and
slide in the roots having first stood them in a bucket of water
for 40 minutes. Then fill in the hole and stamp down to
remove any air pockets and make sure that the roots are 100
per cent in contact with the soil. Putting a length of pipe into
the ground on planting, with the bottom near the roots and the
top poking up just above the soil, means you can give it a very
effective drink in the first few years so that it doesn't get
stressed in a drought. The advantage of the pipe is that the
water goes straight where it's needed, and doesn't run off the
surface and/or quickly evaporate.

Always flick out the roots, pointing them in every direction,
and make sure that the base of the trunk is at soil level
(another way of checking the right planting level is to check
that the point where the highest roots shoot out is flush with
the ground).

The immediate area must be completely clear from
competing growth (especially grass and weeds), leaving bare
soil. Get rid of the competition. Then water and add a thick
organic mulch (keeping it clear of the trunk) to stop the
moisture quickly evaporating.

For what are called ornamental trees you'll need to be
slightly more precious. Dig a hole about three times the
diameter of the root system, and about 30cm (1ft) deep. On
hard ground prang up the bottom with a fork, but don't start
digging for coal because 90 per cent of the roots won't go any
deeper than this. There's also the danger that if you dig a big
hole packed with organic matter the tree will slowly sink into
it – a wet winter pit – and die a slow, rotting death.

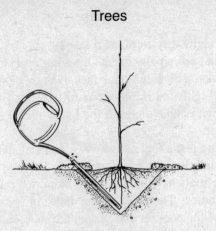

Fig. 6. How to plant a tree.

Tall trees over 1.8m (6ft) need staking for just over a year to keep them upright. Hammer a stout stake into the ground so that it's pointing at 45 degrees into the prevailing wind and reaches just past the trunk. Secure the two with a tree tie – never use rope or string – and keep checking that the tie isn't cutting into the wood. And that's it. Except . . .

Mycorrhizal fungi

Give young trees a fighting start. Dab Mycorrhizal fungi on the tree's roots on planting (or put one teaspoon in the planting hole) and you'll be giving them an extra dose of what happens in nature: a two-way mutually beneficial relationship. The trees feed the fungi and the fungi help the trees' roots absorb more water and nutrients. And this makes young trees grow strongly and helps them withstand everything from drought to disease. In short, you'd be mad not to use it. In most soils trees acquire this fungi, but it can take from three to five years. Why wait?

Tree topiary and American websites
Q: Why do shrubs get topiarized but not trees?
A: Because it's gone right out of fashion but . . .

Google American and Australian websites, especially *www.arborsmith.com* and *www.pooktree.com*, and you'll see

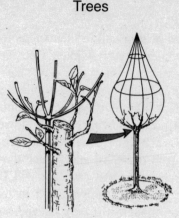

Fig. 7. How to train a fruit tree.

how tweakers, twisters and pruners are using saplings to grow
stick people, barns and boats and even four-legged trees (see
Tricks With Trees, Pavilion, 2007).

Fruit trees are regularly topiarized and trained into goblets,
cylinders and pyramids, giving a fun, geometric shape with
extra thickets of fruit in a small space. Try growing an upright
apple tree with an M26 rootstock, which restricts the final
height to about 2.7m (9ft), and nip out the top of the stem
(Fig. 7) to generate a batch of side shoots at the top. The top
four can be trained around a large metal template shaped like
a giant tear. Once you've tried that, experiment.

The key points are that (a) stopping (nipping back the growing
tip) of a young tree stem makes it fire out new replacement
shoots which you can train anywhichway especially because
(b) the new growth is far bendier than you'd imagine, and can
easily be bent into arches and circles, and (c) when two stems are
bound together they will, in time, fuse together or inosculate,
producing a permanent, solid join. Train trees to produce not just
a traditional mushroom head or ball but elaborate gothic
structures (*see* Ivan Hicks in Contemporary gardens, page 39).

Tackling overgrown trees
You've got two choices with a tree that's outgrowing its space,

and that's get rid of it or call in the experts to thin and cut it back in late summer or early winter. Trees grow on average 30cm (1ft) a year, so a new one will take many years to provide the same shelter and privacy unless you're growing amazing sprinters like eucalyptus. If thinning, "lift the crown", which means sawing off the lower branches to radically increase the light levels beneath. You can also thin the crown by up to one-third and reduce the length of long branches. But remember that each cut will fire out a fuzzy burst of new replacement growth, and in turn that'll need constant pruning, though it'll be a cheaper, quicker job. To saw off branches see pages 26–7.

Coppicing and pollarding

Trees do exactly what humans can't – grow replacement limbs. When a stag chomps through the tip of a sapling, the sapling regenerates and retaliates by sending out new shoots from the top. Early hairy people must have seen this happen, and realized that the new lengths were ideal for making poles, spears, firewood and fences. So simply cut back the likes of a young alder (*Alnus*), ash (*Fraxinus*), birch (*Betula),* elm (*Ulmus*), hazel (*Corylus*), oak (*Quercus*) and willow (*Salix*) just above ground level in late winter/early spring (and early spring means "early" not "late", when the tree might have had its burst of growth). Once done, you must keep coppicing – though ash, hazel and oak can be cut back more infrequently to give thicker wood – or you'll end up with a stump firing out a bizarre clump of ever-thickening branches with heavy shade beneath. The good news is that regular coppicing prolongs the life of the tree because it has to keep regenerating itself. It also creates multi-stemmed trees and a woodland look, and guarantees that you keep getting the new brightly coloured stems on the likes of a dogwood (*Cornus*). If left for a few years, this bright colour starts to muddy and fade. Multi-stemmed white birches are amazing.

Pollarding is no different but you make the cut about head

high, and this protects the crop of new shoots from grazing animals. With repeated pollarding (and once you've started, you've got to carry on or you'll end up with a one-off fattening, thickening clutter of overweight poles) the trunk develops a thick head. Don't try cutting back a conifer or you'll kill it. Good contenders include young acers, ash, common limes (*Tilia* x *europaea*), elms (*Ulmus*), London planes (*Platanus* x *hispanica*) and willows. Mature trees don't respond well to coppicing or pollarding, and might get infections and/or rot. Many die.

The best conifers (and that's not a contradiction)

Conifers get a sniffy, snooty press. "They don't do anything." But (1) they're bullet-proof, hardy and evergreen, (2) provide superb protection for birds in winter, (3) offer height and bulk, giving good privacy and windbreaks, and (4) add colours, including bluish-lilac and rich green, and even changing winter-summer colours on the same plant. And if you want to amend the shape, get pruning, but never cut back hard into old wood or you'll be left with a bare gappy toothy hole because they won't reshoot from old wood.

A quick rundown goes like this. Choose from 60 species and 2,000 forms. Sizes range from the tallest sequoias to the 15 x 15cm (6 x 6in) incredibly hard, dense oval *Cryptomeria japonica* 'Tenzan-sugi' like a bright green tortoise with *rigor mortis*, excellent for *saikei*, creating a miniaturized Japanese landscape. For tall thin exclamation marks try *Juniperus communis* 'Sentinel', and the blue-green *J. scopulorum* 'Skyrocket'. For silver-blue you need *J. s.* 'Gray Gleam'. The Irish have their dark green recent find, *Taxus baccata* 'Fastigiata Robusta', and the Italians *Cupressus sempervirens* 'Stricta', but beware of frosts when young. And if you've got a garden the size of Ohio, and want great magical organ pipes, 27m (90ft) high, buy a multi-stemmed *Calocedrus decurrens*, all reddish-brown bark.

Midget conifers can make amazingly tight tactile mounds.

Barnacle them over a rockery, flank them beside a path or zigzag them across open gravel. Two of the best are *Picea abies* 'Little Gem' at 30 x 30cm (12 x 12in) and *Thuja occidentalis* 'Danica'. And if you want something crinkly tufty and rare, track down the slightly bigger *Larix kaempferi* 'Nana' at the price of an excellent Pinot Gris.

Now the monsters. Not staggering great growths but spooks. Give *Cedrus deodora* 'Gold Mound' a few judicious cuts and you've got Freddy Krueger with his ragged slouch hat, old pullover and metal gloves tipped with flashing knives. Light that up at night. *C. libani atlantica* 'Glauca Pendula' wants to be a massive, great thrusting out sprawler and makes a terrific cave under its branches, but you can whip it into shape and train it into an arch.

Other goodies? *Abies procera* 'Glauca Prostrata', which bobbles across ground for 1.2m (4ft) like a string of bright blue sausages. Keep snipping off any skyward shoots. *Picea glauca* 'J. W. Daisy's White' is a compact cone, cream-white in spring and green in late summer. *Chamaecyparis thyoides* 'Rubicon' turns silver purple in cold winter snaps. And *Cryptomeria japonica* 'Elegans', ridiculously rarely grown, has thick, flaking, orange-red bark and new leaves turning reddish-bronze in the cold.

For whacking big cones try silver firs (*Abies*), often ripening from white to blue, especially the 14cm (5in) long ones of *Abies concolor, A. forrestii* – 15cm (6in), *A. nordmanniana* – 18cm (7in), and *A. procera* – up to 25cm (10in). Note the cones often appear and break up high up on tall trees, dispersing seed on the wind. With spruce, eg *Picea breweriana* – 10cm (4in) long – the brown cones fall complete.

Christmas trees and what to do with them

The best trees grow in the garden and stay there. If you must stand a Christmas tree indoors, it's odds on you'll have bought a Norway spruce (*Picea abies*) though you'd be better off looking for an *Abies* or *Pinus* (especially *P. sylvestris*) if you don't want a needlefest on the carpet. Special sprays might help but ...

Buy one in a pot with a good root system and then you can give it regular drinks and keep it happyish, though being indoors near a radiator or log fire is crazy. The briefer its frazzling period in the dry heat of a modern house, the better. Ten days, no more. Most trees don't come with roots, but they still need drinks. Saw off the bottom 12mm (½in) or take out a wedge (this is vital because a felled tree seals over the cut with sap, and it can't drink until this cap has been removed), and stand the tree in a bucket packed with pebbles or rocks to stabilize it, and then top up with water. Keep an eye on the level because it can drink a couple of pints a day. Bare-root trees can be potted up (again, give good drinks when required).

If the rooted, pot-growing tree is going to be planted outside and brought in again next year, it'll need heavy 'lerv'. (It's a better bet than a bare-root tree which will never have that good a root system.) Keep misting it with water so that the leaves don't dry out too much, and don't rush to get it outside if the weather is so severe that the tree will go into shock. Wait until the frosts, floods or gales have gone. Meantime, stand it in a cool, sheltered place (eg the garage). Plant outside in a largish pot, with big holes in the bottom, to restrict its growth.

The winter garden (that's autumn to spring)

If you haven't got a garden the size of Albania, you can only pick a few trees, so check they're multipurpose. The five categories are bark, spring blossom, autumn leaves, berries and extra tricks. If you plant trees in threes, with two in the foreground, set wide apart, and the third between and behind, the eye is immediately propelled into the gap, suggesting extra distance.

Trees with smart bark (the shopping list) ...
Acers – the snakebark maple (*A. griseum*) looks like it has been

trashed by a loony with a potato peeler because the cinnamon bark is constantly peeling off. Give it acid soil. A good autumn show with orange, red and scarlet. *A. pensylvanicum* 'Erythrocladum' has pink winter shoots and yellow stripes, turning orange-red and white, with yellow autumn leaves. Not a strong grower and best kept as a shrub. *A. palmatum* 'Sango-kaku' has thrilling lobster pinkish-red young stems in winter and orange-yellow autumn leaves. Indispensable, but you can go one better (see *Polyepis australis*).

Arbutus x *andrachnoides* – the Shane Warne of evergreens. Sumptuous reddish-brown peeling bark gives brighter patches of colour, clusters of white flowers and orange-red vile-tasting fruit. Multipurpose. If it's open-headed 8m (25ft) height is too big try 'Elfin King' at 2.5m (8ft).

Arctostaphylos manzanita – dark red-brown bark and a real beauty with twisty, see-though branches at just 4m (12ft) high and wide. But it does need acid soil.

Birches – the whites ones, especially the ubiquitous *Betula utilis* var. *jacquemontii* and the even better 'Jermyns'. Both the long, lean single-stemmed and the multi-stemmed kind are highly effective in groves or an immaculate circle highlighting a feature within. Keep the lower trunks clean of mud-splash with an occasional hose down or a bucket of warm water and detergent. Bright yellow autumn leaves. The peeling river birch (*B. nigra*) has reddish-brown bark, while the self-stripping *B. albosinensis* var. *septentrionalis* is orange-grey and copper.

Eucalyptus pauciflora niphophila – the Australian snow gum is a whopper of a tall, lean angular white that keeps shedding strips of bark. Underneath you get fantastic patterned patches of cinnamon, green and cream. *E. viminalis* also has white bark and *E. urnigera* is cream, grey and white. Some are manic growers, putting on 1.8m (6ft) a year.

Luma apiculata – flaking cinnamon bark revealing patches of white, with late summer flowers and purple fruit (in a good year). Mild gardens only.

Polyepis australis – the shaggiest, most manic stripper, and if you thought the *Acer* was mad, try this. A semi-evergreen shrub which won't get more than 3m (9ft) high, and slightly wider, with great all-over lengths of peeling cinnamon bark. There's one growing at the Sir Harold Hillier Gardens in Hampshire and one at Nymans Garden in West Sussex. From mountainous Argentina, not Australia, where it's one of the few genera to form patches of forest at high altitudes. Often found in ravines. Needs a sheltered position.

Prunus serrula – the Indispensable No. 1. Shiny mahogany brown flaking bark – totally strokable – with striking horizontal bands of lenticels (raised pores). An OK show of spring flowers and yellowish autumn leaves. Coppice it every five years to a 60cm (2ft) high stem because the young growth, when broom-stick thick, has the best colour. *P. rufa*, found by Roy Lancaster in the Himalayas in the 1970s, flakes even more.

Rhododendron barbatum and *R. thomsonii* – two striking rhodos, between a small tree and a spreading shrub, getting 6m (20ft) high. *R. barbatum* has rich, shiny, reddish-purple peeling bark. Scarlet flowers in early spring. *R. thompsonii* has peeling cinnamon bark and blood red mid-spring flowers but can get powdery mildew. Both need acid soil and a sheltered site. The fattening flower buds are incredibly susceptible to winter frost.

Rubus cockburnianus – not a tree but a thicket of a deciduous 2.5m (8ft) high shrub which looks like it has been sprayed with Tippex because it has a white covering in winter. Good contrast with the small black evergreen *Ophiopogon planis-capus* 'Nigrescens' and red dogwoods (see opposite). The much harder to find and less vigorous *R. peltatus* gets 90cm (3ft) high and has purple stems with a white covering.

Sequoia sempervirens and *Sequoiadendron giganteum* – two high-octane thumping fat telegraph poles with padded, spongy, reddish-brown bark. Don't let children peel them.

Stewartia pseudocamellia – the bark is a mix of peeling dull orange-brown and patches of bright orange. Also midsummer white flowers and red autumn leaves.

Tilia platyphyllos 'Rubra' – a lime bristling with a fuzz of red twigs. Bring on the snow. Pollard for the best effect.

Spring flowers/blossom
Amelanchier lamarckii – a feisty show of white spring flowers on a small tree followed by black fruit, and autumn reds and orange. Also try *A.* x *grandiflora* 'Ballerina'.

Cercis siliquastrum – the Judas tree, a spectacular street sight in Portugal and Spain where the long scorching summers generate thickets of magenta-pink flowers in spring. Otherwise . . .

Crab apple (*Malus*) – abundant bursts of blossom followed by small, inedible fruit (see page 66).

Dogwood (*Cornus*) – two North Americans with a white pillow-burst explosion in spring are *C. florida* and *C. nuttallii*, but the former is best in the southern half of the UK. The two helped parent the exquisite 'Eddie's White Wonder', which is the one to get, followed by 'Ormonde'. Both have good autumn colours.

Handkerchief tree (*Davidia involucrata*) – in late spring it's covered by thousands of white bracts (the flowers are actually tiny). Hardly handkerchiefs but incredibly impressive.

Hawthorn (*Crataegus*) – rough-tough indestructible trees with late spring white flowers and berries for the birds.

Laburnum x *watereri* 'Vossii' – dangles massed thickets of yellow flowers, up to 60cm (2ft) long. Plant a lengthy tunnel of absolute magic with purple alliums reaching up to touch the yellow. Made famous by Rosemary Verey.

Lilac (*Syringa*) – many are smallish, about 4m (13ft) high with two pinks, *Syringa* x *josiflexa* 'Bellicent' and *S. sweginzowii*, top of the list; heaven in late spring. *S. microphylla* 'Superba' is a shrub, about 1.2m (4ft) high with large pink flowers and keeps on flowering, in bursts, through summer.

Magnolia – *M. tripetala* gets ignored but it has mega (deciduous) leaves, over 30cm (12in) long, and late spring white flowers. They initially sit up and then splay open. It has tropical looks, is extremely hardy and is a rare magnolia because it pongs. It has bright red cones, the leaves colour up nicely before falling and you can apparently chew the bark like tobacco. Three-in-one. For good late spring scent you need the multi-stemmed 'Charles Coates', 'Nimbus' (probably the strongest scent) or *M. obovata* which is really quick growing when young, shooting 75cm (2½ft) a year with 45cm (18in) long leaves if you're lucky. *M. sieboldii* has bright white flowers which, unusually for a magnolia, hang down, with rich red anthers, a lovely evening whiff and is staggeringly hardy, making it *de rigueur* in Japanese gardens. The multi-stemmed shrub *M. wilsonii* also has hanging-down flowers, all the better for getting your nose in.

The big problem with all of them is that they can get slayed by late spring frosts; one savage night and that's it. A 12-month wait 'til next year. So grow them in sunny, sheltered sites, and that shelter is important because they hate being hit by cold, strong winds. Most are woodland plants. All like a thick spring mulch to keep the roots cool and moist, slightly acidic soil, except for *M. wilsonii*. Or, far more sensibly, choose a summer-flowering magnolia like *M.* x *wieseneri* with its fruity scent. If you want one which flowers in late winter, but without any scent, go for *M. campbellii* or one of its cultivars. And if you live in the far south-west, with your toes in the Gulf Stream, get *M.* 'Trewidden Belle', a terrible name for a pink beauty flowering in January.

Prunus – the completely unfussy ornamental cherry is unbeatable for a mid-air blossom explosion. Try *P.* 'Accolade', *P. avium* 'Plena' (even on chalk), *P.* 'Kursar', *P. sargentii* 'Rancho' also for good autumn colour, and the Japanese cherries with *P.* 'Kanzan', 'Shirofugen', 'Shirotae', 'Shogetsu' and 'Taihaku' high on the list. But note some cherries are terrific whoppers, getting 10m (30ft) wide and even taller. If you want a good midget go for *P. incisa* 'Kojo-no-mai'. It's 2.5m (8ft) high and wide and one of the first to flower; delicate, not brash.

Rhododendron – where to start? The choice is so huge (850 species and 25,000 cultivars) with heights going up to 10m (30ft) and colours from white to red and yellow, making great flowery skyscrapers, you've got to visit a specialist nursery before buying. You'll need acid soil, dappled shade and shelter from cold winds. Beware when tidying up around one because they are surface rooting, which means you can't start digging around the trunk because you'll damage the roots. Mulch to keep the roots cool.

Sorbus megalocarpa – dense clusters of white flowers at the start of spring, followed by brown berries. The other excellent sorbuses tend to flower towards the end of spring, and many have flashier, brighter berries (see page 67).

Autumn leaves
Acer palmatum – fizzing with reds and yellows. The shrubby Dissectum group has finely divided leaves. All need shelter

from icy winds. Old plants look like wizened hunchbacks. Visit a specialist nursery.

Liquidambars – vertical firebrands, especially from the many forms of *L. styraciflua* (eg 'Lane Roberts' and 'Worplesdon'). *L. s.* 'Gumball' and 'Oconee' are rounded midgets at 2m (6ft).

Nyssa sylvatica – more orange/yellow/red foliage.

Also try *Amelanchier lamarckii*, beech (*Fagus*), birches (*Betula*) which invariably need staking for their first year because they have shallow roots, cherries (*Prunus*), *Cornus kousa* var. *chinensis*, crab apples (*Malus*), hawthorn (*Crataegus*), hornbeams (*Carpinus*), horse chestnuts (*Aesculus*), *Nothofagus*, *Nyssa*, oak (*Quercus*), *Parrotia persica*, poplar (*Populus*), *Sorbus* and *Stewartia*. Just one stag's horn sumach (*Rhus typhina*) can quickly create a small thicket because it spreads by underground suckers, but rip away the new growth where it joins the parent and it won't multiply.

Berries/fruit

Cotoneasters – fail-safe, robust cotoneasters come in all sizes, from trees to shrubs. Make the right choice and you'll get typically white or pink flowers (the earliest in April) and loads of September to December fruit in red, yellow, orange, black, white, pink or even violet hanging on all winter, into the following spring. *C. frigidus* 'Cornubia' is the top tip.

Crab apple (*Malus*) – huge range, the best with modest height, spring blossom, autumn leaves and small, striking, totally inedible fruit. 'Red Sentinel' has red fruit and *M. tschonoskii* an orange-red-purple autumn flare up.

Holly (*Ilex*) – fruiting hollies come in red, yellow and black. You'll need a female and a nearby male, but ignore the names because some sexually challenged berk came up with 'Golden Queen' for a male and 'Golden King' for a female. Or get a self-pollinating evergreen female like 'J. C. van Tol'. If you really want the winter berries to stand out, get the deciduous *I. verticillata* 'Winter Red' because the bare branches are barnacled with bright red berries.

Sorbus – *S. aucuparia* has orange-red berries that'll hang on well into the New Year. *S.* 'Joseph Rock' is a great yellow, *S. cashmiriana* white and *S. commixta* 'Embley' scarlet, all with a big bang of autumn colour. Select with care. Some berry so early that the birds gulp down the lot before winter.

Also try hawthorn (*Crataegus*) and strawberry tree (*Arbutus unedo*).

Extra tricks
Cercidiphyllum japonicum – when the leaves redden and drop in autumn there's a powerful whiff of toffee apples and burnt sugar and you can smell it from 6m (20ft) away. Otherwise unremarkable, but that smell.

Corylus avellana 'Contorta' – the corkscrew hazel makes squiggly aerial tracery; highly effective against the winter sky. Thin out to avoid massive congestion.

Eucalyptus gunnii – coppice to keep generating the young blue foliage.

Gleditsia triacanthos – produces curvy-twisted seed pods up to 45cm (18in) long which rattle in the wind. Spiny trunk.

Paulownia tomentosa – when coppiced all its energy is channelled into the few leaves, but they can get a flapping 90cm (3ft) wide.

Architectural/high-performance trees (and shrubs)
Gardens need ornamental toughies so that when all the happy-flowery kind are underground in winter, they're out there chesting the winds. The following is just an indication.

Alnus cordata – one of the unfussiest trees around, the Italian alder grows virtually anywhere, even in the damp, and on chalk. Superb when dangling catkins. Glossy green leaves. *A.* x *spaethii* also has an excellent show of winter catkins.

Bay (*Laurus nobilis*) – bay needs quick-draining soil and areas with low rainfall, and if you can guarantee that you can grow a very impressive hedge.

Brachyglottis – *B. repanda* x *greyi* has large flopsy leaves, just short of 30cm (12in) long, light grey on top and silvery underneath. Cut off the summer flowers the moment they appear so that the plant puts all its energy into making bigger leaves. *B. monroi* has much shorter, olive-green foliage.

Dogwood (*Cornus alba* 'Sibirica') – totally essential because of the stunning, striking red winter stems. Keep coppicing, cutting right back each spring, because the new stems have the best coloured bark. Without coppicing the stems quite quickly lose the bright red; it becomes watered down, mudddyish-brown. With large plants you could cut back half the stems one year, the other half the next. Also try *C. sanguinea* 'Winter Beauty' and 'Midwinter Fire'. Plant different coloured forms right next to each other, with *C. sericea* 'Flaviramea' (yellow-green) and *C. alba* 'Kesselringii' (blackish-purple), but hold them up next to each other in the nursery to check the colour scheme. The red ones make a snappy midwinter clash against white-barked betulas.

Eriobotrya japonica – in the mildest areas it makes a tree but even as a shrub you get 30cm (12in) long, evergreen leaves, green and crinkly on top, woolly beneath. Exotic chic. The loquat needs a sheltered inner city garden where the temperature won't dip much below −3°C (27°F). Feed in late spring.

Magnolia grandiflora – it grows like a weed in Italy but will thrive in the colder UK, against a protected sunny wall. Needs a setting to match its magnificence. Shiny bright leaves 20cm (8in) long, matched by the whacking big 25cm (10in) wide flowers. 'Goliath' and 'Exmouth' are the top choices in the UK with open flowers from midsummer to autumn.

Monkey puzzle (*Araucaria araucana*) – you need a finely tuned eye because the monkey puzzle can easily be extremely odd. Where are *you* going to stick it? Has razor-tipped needles at the ends of the leaves. Spectacularly sharp. In theory it needs plenty of space but growing at an average 18cm (7in) a year, it'll be the next century before one planted today hits 15m (50ft).

Pinus montezumae – joyous in the morning sun with zillions of highly tactile grass-like leaves dangling a good 25cm (10in) long. Slow growing, so ignore the eventual height. You'll be long gone before it hits 24m (80ft). Needs shelter. Or try the Mexican weeping pine (*P. patula*).

Prunus x *subhirtella* 'Autumnalis' – a medium-sized winter cherry with sporadic pinkish-white flowers right through midwinter; being sporadic makes them even more of a treat. 'Pendula Plena Rosea' is the weeping form.

Rosmarinus 'Miss Jessops Upright' – the surprise choice. An upright shrub with a very decent shape, getting 2m (6ft) high and wide. If it gets too cluttered and blobby, keep opening it up, pruning, sculpting. Even the bog standard *R. officinalis* can be styled into a sexy little beast.

Teucrium fruticans – bushy evergreen snipped into globes.

Trachycarpus fortunei – huge open fans of leaves about 60cm (2ft) wide, held clear of the shaggy trunk on long stalks. The hardiest palm. Keep away from flaying winds which ruin its looks.

See also – bamboos and conifers (good colours and strong shapes), Trees with smart bark (page 60), crab apples (*Malus* 'Comtesse de Paris' because it's medium size and the yellow berries hang on well after Christmas) and sorbus (page 67).

Topiary

Some trees and shrubs are the ultimate *blobmeister*, but you can easily smarten them up. Forget clichéd, monogenetic peacocks; on the bonfire. Pile 'em up. You want wit. Imagination. Fun.

Start with weepers like *Pyrus salicifolia* 'Pendula'; they can be given a stunningly airy, elegant hairstyle. You'd never think it – a spaghetti-storm of tangled growth – but start with a plant when it is shoulder height and you can keep a clean, single trunk with its wig erupting from the top, giving arching, see-through growth. Relentless thinning and pruning is essential, and keeping the topgrowth in proportion to the leg. *Ceanothus thyrsiflorus* can also be upgraded into a weeping tree a good 4.5m (15ft) high, packed with blue flowers in spring, and glossy evergreen leaves and greenish bark. Other evergreen shrubs with stout supporting trunks can be shaved low down so that all the greenery is raised up, becoming a block of green on legs. There's no diagram, no blueprint. Get out; get snipping.

For traditional topiary, you need one small-leaved evergreen, which is why everyone goes on about box or *Lonicera nitida*. Don't be smart and use large leaves because you'll have to cut through them and the project is a fiasco of disfigurement before you've even started. Once you've bought a plant – the larger and bushier the better but you can also buy several small cheap ones and grow them to the height you want before you start cutting, giving regular trims each summer to make them even bushier, knowing you've got replacements lined up if/when you make a fist of it – think hard about designs. Google the RHS for (standard, very effective, you've-seen it-all-before classical) topiary.

To cut a top-to-bottom spiral, tie a piece of string at the top and wind it around and down to the bottom so that you've got a line to follow. (There, you know how to do it, but all gardening should be a jihad against cliché.) More ambitious geometric shapes give extra welly. You can even snip out a Henry Moore/Barbara Hepworth evergreen sculpture (Google both for images). Or try a lopsided alien, or a neck sticking out of the ground with a pop-eyed head. Or make a large piece of topiary from lots of smaller Lego-type plants, growing them all in pots. A very pukka lady who runs a box nursery once told me she made a 13ft-racing car for a chap who played in Pink Floyd. She used big yellow blobs for the wheels and the body was racing green. They drove 50 plants up to Hampstead and cut them to shape on the spot. And if you're wondering why big pieces of box are so expensive, it's because nurserymen have got to use, say, large 10-year old plants – and box grows very slowly, just 15cm (6in) a year – so they take quite a bit of looking after. You're not just buying the shaping but the 10-years' worth of care.

Make sure you give box an annual spring feed of seaweed fertilizer to keep it strong and healthy, and trim twice a year, in spring and late summer. If it snows, knock it off quick before the shape is squashed. And if growing topiary in a pot, note that it'll still need a drink after it has rained because the drops invariably bounce off the head, which acts like an umbrella.

5

CLIMBERS AND SHRUBS

The up-there garden

Don't miss a trick. Keep the eye pinging about. Everything up-there is an empty box or aerial flower bed. Fill it. Grow climbers up walls, training them up rows of horizontal wires set every 20–25cm (8–10in) apart. The wire is stretched tautly between galvanized vine eyes (they're long screws with a ring at the end to which you attach the wire). Also hammer up arches and arbours, cool, shady places to sit out in summer with a wooden structure or canopy overhead holding up the climbers. Make tripods and wigwams about 1.5m (5ft) high. Use dead oaks as climbing frames (but beware the quick-decaying dead because they will become unstable and can quickly collapse in a gale). Anything (even trellis) for climbers to wriggle up. All you've got to do is make sure that climbers have an artificial or plant support system onto which they can cling. And never plant them flush to the base of the wall because they won't get enough rain. Plant them a good 45–60cm (18–24in) away, angled towards the wall, giving the roots more rain and space to roam.

Climbers climb cleverly. Some use their leaf stalks to grab onto structures and tightly twist around them. Others have long tendrils, like mini lassoos, which wrap around absolutely anything (even other stems on the same plant). Many use their growing stems to twine in a (usually) clockwise motion around a structure. Roses use their anchoring thorns to clamber up other climbers. And then you get the 'stickers'. Look closely at ivy (*Hedera*) and you'll see zillions of tiny hair-like brown roots, not below ground, but shooting out sideways from the growing, lengthening stems. They clamp on to walls and rocks, and even if you can rip off the ivy stems, the roots nearly always get left behind. Climbers like Virginia creeper (*Parthenocissus*) have mini suction pads which lock onto surfaces like Spiderwoman going up a skyscraper.

The walls are OK but not the roof

Climbers are fine against walls but check they're in good shape. Climbers won't initiate problems, but they can definitely exacerbate them. Then nail up support wires and, given a long enough ladder and enough time, you can control their growth but don't let them on the roof where they can cause hideous, expensive damage, prising off the roof tiles.

Scented climbers

Clematis armandii – erupting lengths of growth with pinkish-creamy flowers in spring and a gentle waft of scent. Needs hot sun and shelter from frosts and flaying cold winds because the strikingly finger-like evergreen leaves, grouped in threes, get ruined. The leaves give good cover being 15cm (6in) long. Ignore all the Group 1, 2 and 3 pruning advice in books for other clematis because it doesn't apply. Chop back when it's getting OTT. 6m (20ft) – all the following are likely maximum heights if they're grown in the right conditions.

Clematis flammula – a deciduous rampant climber with absolutely massive outpourings of tiny white flowers in late summer with a heady scent. 7.5m (25ft)

Clematis 'Mayleen' – plenty of vigorous growth and tiny pink mid-spring flowers with a vanilla scent. 6m (20ft)

Clematis montana – also deciduous, with more vanilla in spring when grown in a sheltered hotspot. 6m (20ft)

Holboellia coriacea – a Chinese evergreen found in 1907 by E. H. Wilson with clustered greenish-white female flowers and purple-green males. The strongest scent from a hardy vine. You can whiff it 5.5m (18ft) away. Another climber queuing up for that sunny, sheltered wall. 6m (20ft)

Honeysuckle *(Lonicera)* – find a specialist honeysuckle nursery and do a sniff test. Try *L. similis* var. *delavayi* (flowering late spring until late summer and beyond), *L.* x *americana, L. caprifolium, L. japonica* 'Halliana' and common honeysuckle (*L. periclymenum*). Powerful fruity scents carrying across the garden.

Jasminum officinale – give it plenty of room and sun because when happy it is prodigious, lashing everywhichway shoots. A mix of white summer flowers with major pongs and evergreen/deciduous leaves (they hang on in mild winters, fall when it's bad). Grow against a house wall, training it around open windows or through a tall, twiggy hedge or up an arch, but you can't cut back until after flowering or you'll lose the show. *J. o.* f. *affine* has slightly larger flowers and 'Inverleith' dark red buds giving white flowers, red stripes on the back. 12m (40ft)

Roses – where to start? All those listed have strong scent and good colour, but those with an (R) are ramblers. The difference? Climbers include all kinds of roses, from hybrid teas to old garden roses, with different flower shapes. Many flower all summer into autumn. The stems become stiff, sturdy and rigid and the new shoots are best trained around a post or out horizon-tally, to either side, because that'll generate more shoots from low down and extra flowers – not just right up-there but here, at nose level. Vigorous ramblers have long, bendy, firing-up stems and are usually launched up, against and over garden structures, or even into trees. Most flower once a season, usually with a mega display in the first part of summer.

REDS
'Château de Clos-Vougeot, Climbing'
'Crimson Glory'
'Ena Harkness, Climbing'
'Etoile de Holland'
'Guinée'
'Souvenir de Claudius Denoyel'

WHITES
'Albéric Barbier' (R)
'Bobbie James' (R)
'Francis E. Lester' (R)
'Madame Alfred Carrière'
'Rambling Rector' (R), which is virtually identical to . . .
'Seagull' (R)
'Wedding Day' (R)

YELLOWS
'Dreaming Spires'
'Gloire de Dijon'
'Lady Hillingdon, Climbing'
'Maigold'

PINKS
'Aloha'
'Blush Noisette'
'Constance Spry'
'Kathleen Harrop'
'Madame Grégoire Staechelin'
'New Dawn'
'Paul's Himalayan Musk' (R), and one more on the next page . . .

'Zéphirine Drouhin', provided you remember to spray it against blackspot, mildew and you name it.

Sweet peas (*Lathyrus*) – grow them up cane wigwams or nets for runner beans, and make sure you buy the highly, powerfully scented kind like *L. grandiflora* 'America' and 'Matucana' and *L. odoratus* 'Painted Lady and 'Cream Southbourne'. All can be grown from seed, but you need to soak them in tepid water first to accelerate the germinate process. Nip back the young stems to generate extra bushy growth. Midsummer flowering.

Trachelospermum jasminoides – fast-growing twining stems and pure white flowers. (Not as quick as *Pueraria montana* var. *lobata* from the Far East though, an invading overwhelming weed in America which spurts 20m/60ft a year.) Needs a sunny, sheltered site because it's not that hardy. 6m (20ft)

Wisteria – a simple choice between the Chinese (*W. sinensis*) and Japanese (*W. floribunda*) kinds. The Chinese are generally more powerful, and climb higher with larger flowers and richer scent but, and it's a big BUT, they flower in late spring and can easily get zapped by a late frost destroying all the buds. The Japanese are a safer bet in 'iffy' areas because they flower slightly later and miss the frosts. *W. sinensis* 'Alba' is white, and the 'Prolific' blue will start flowering even when knee high. All are sold as grafted plants, but check that there's a healthy graft, so look at the join between what's called the rootstock (the technical word for the roots, the feeding part, the engine) and the topgrowth (the flowering part). The top of the rootstock is the darker wood and is about 23cm (9in) above the soil, and that's joined to the paler topgrowth. Don't take cuttings or grow from seedlings because they might take 20 years to flower, and then they might be rubbish.

Other (weird, whacky and beautiful) climbers
Actinidia kolomikta – a bizarre mix of green, white and pink

leaves. Best in light shade to maintain the colours. 5m (15ft)

Akebia quinata – small, distinctive brownish-purple flowers and sausage-like fruit in a hot summer. 10m (30ft)

Aristolochia grandiflora or *macrophylla* – weird flowers like a smoker's pipe with a U-bend in the middle and large leaves. Conservatories only. 8m (25ft)

Campsis radicans or *C*. x *tagliabuana* 'Mme Galen' heat-loving vigorous vine with flashy orange-red clustered flowers. 7.5m (25ft)

Clematis – too many to mention, but go for one like *C. tangutica* with large spidery seedheads after the flowers, like silver hair flapping out of an armpit. *C. cirrhosa* var. *balearica* flowers in winter with paprika spotted pale cream flowers. 3m (10ft)

Clianthus puniceus – woody shrub with dangling giant red flowers, but not totally hardy. 4m (12ft)

Cobaea scandens – massively rampant annual. Grow from seed and it'll easily cover a wall in summer with large cream-green flowers, 5cm (2in) long and wide, turning purple. 5m (15ft)

Eccremocarpus scaber – excellent results in a sheltered hotspot with fresh green small leaves and trailing growth bursting with rich orange-red flowers. After a few years it dies but so what? Get another. Easily grown from seed. 5m (15ft)

Ipomoea – some of the richest colours, especially 'Grandpa Otts' (violet-blue), 'Kniola's Black' (deep rich bluish-purple) and 'Scarlett O'Hara' (scarlet). Grow from seed. 2.4m (8ft)

Lapageria rosea – given a mild climate, shelter and cool shade (it comes from Chilean woods), it'll be thick with sumptuously beautiful, fleshy, dangling red flowers from mid-summer set against dark green leaves. 5m (15ft)

Parthenocissus quinquefolia – an autumn blast of Virginia creeper with thumping wine red leaves. It clamps up a wall thanks to mini suckers, so make sure that the surface is in excellent shape before planting. Or grow into a stout old useless tree. 15m (50ft)

Passiflora caerulea – the typical choice, with 10cm (4in) wide white flowers but they are slightly mad and freakish with a ring of blue 'hairs' set against the white petals, and there's a protruding stalk in the centre. In belting good summers it produces egg-shaped fruit. Excellent drainage, shelter and sun. 10m (30ft)

Rhodochiton atrosanguineum – another whacky climber with purple flowers like descending, open parachutes, and phallic maroon tubes dangling out the bottom. Grow from seed. 3m (10ft)

Schisandra rubriflora – clusters of red flowers in spring, and if you grow two (male and female) you'll get red berries. 10m (30ft)

Solanum crispum 'Glasnevin' – prolific, totally prolific, with blue flowers. 6m (20ft)

Tropaeolum – bright red nasturtiums for letting rip through hedges or up wigwams. *T. majus* (in red, yellow and orange) is an annual easily grown from seed; *T. speciosum* (bright red) grows from a rhizome and *T. tuberosum* (orange-red and yellow) from a tuber. 2.4m (8ft) and more

Vitis coignetiae – not the *Vitis* for tasty grapes but grown for its gigantic spread which can paint the side of a house bright red for a few weeks in autumn. 12m (40ft)

How to grow bush roses

First, why roses? Because one or two provide rich colours and get-close scents; not from 3m (10ft) away, you've got to get your nose in. If you've a large garden for big shrub roses, even rose hedges, great. In a small garden, just one hybrid tea, with perfectly shaped, pointed, fat swelling buds is an event in itself. If you grow one which does not flower that prolifically, it's even more special. Like *R*. 'Papa Meilland'. The blood red buds, fatten and do everything but open, and for days nothing happens . . . Nothing nothing nothing then Woompf the petals fling back and the eye is open, open and ready and you can cup it in your hand and bend to inhale a scent that'll rock your mind.

Before planting a new hybrid tea, prune if it's the bare-root kind (ie bought from late autumn to late winter by mail order, when you get a set of long bare dormant twigs and unruly roots), to scare it into making plenty of new growth. Cut back hard to about 15cm (6in) or leave five buds (Fig. 8), and this will force out new replacement shoots low down, building up plenty of strong flowering growth for the future. Also snip off any damaged or really spindly wood – you don't need that – or crossing twigs which are going to bang and rub against each other. Thereafter, at the end of winter, prune the majority

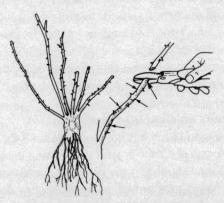

Fig. 8. How to prune a hybrid tea rose.

strong stems to leave about five buds, and weaker growth to leave just three buds.

Pruning – a quick note – isn't just about concentrating the plant's energy into a certain number of strong-growing stems (and getting rid of old dead wood and feeble twigs), but making sure that it fires out new growth where you want it to go. You've got to propel it away from the plant and not into the centre, so when pruning make sure that the top bud is always pointing out. Thereafter, most shrub roses can be left for several years to build up a decent thicket of growth, when you just take out the old wood to instigate new shoots from the base.

Anyway, once you've given the rose its first prune, dig a planting hole, stick it in and water. That's basically it but there's a bit of ritual . . .

If bare root, stick the roots in a bucket of water for 60 minutes to give it a good drink, or water a pot-grown one bought from a garden centre, then dig the hole when the weather isn't hostile. You're not trying to kill it. Make the hole (Fig. 9) wider than, but as deep as, the root system, spreading out the roots so that they'll set off in different directions. The join between the root system (actually from another rose, which is used to guarantee strong growth, energy and disease-resistance) and the topgrowth (the reason why you bought it, the bit with all the flowers) needs to go just below the surface by about 2.5cm (1in). Add organic matter to the heaped-up excavated soil, then pack it in the sides of the hole, around and between the roots but not beneath. Thump down the soil with your heel to punch out any air pockets, and water. Finished.

And two views on climbing roses

You want them to climb but you don't want all the flowers so high up there you can't see or sniff them. Train the long, bendy stems out to the side and, if they're really bendy, into a semi-circle. This forces new growth to break out low down, giving some flowers at head height. Tie in the growth where required.

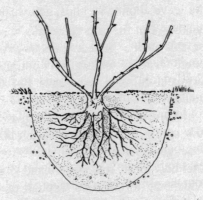

Fig. 9. How to plant a hybrid tea rose.

Or you can prune a climbing rose to leave 15cm (6in) of growth and generate new shoots. And they are then trained to the horizontal. Your choice. Thereafter, nip back the sideshoots when they are packed with dead flowers by two-thirds.

Trying to prune the topgrowth of ramblers growing into trees is bonkers. Leave it. But in winter get rid of (a) any stems that are dying back and (b) no more than one-third of the sound old ones, and that'll encourage new ones to take over. On ornamental structures (like arches), where the rambler growth is completely accessible, you can do both the above and also nip back the sideshoots, after they have flowered, to a young bud. Do this when the main show is over and you'll also get rid of the dead flowers. You're basically getting the plant ready now, in midsummer, for next summer's display.

How to plant shrubs

The same as for a hybrid tea rose, except there's no union between the rootstock and the topgrowth to worry about, so just make sure that it goes into the ground at the same stem depth as before. And make sure it's well watered while getting established with thorough soaks as required, not regular trickles which keep the roots lazily near the surface when you want them plunging deep.

Moving shrubs

Now you're talking. But first, do you *really* want to keep the shrub because this is the perfect time to ditch it and get something better? Or if it's too big, why not just cut it back? Or take replacement cuttings (see pages 124–6). No? Then this is what you do.

Whether evergreen or deciduous, move it from late autumn to early spring. If it's a big mature plant then you'll need to act one year before it's moved. Slice a spade all around the outer edge of its root system and slightly under it, the whole point being to cut right through the hard, tough, thick roots. This circle needs to be a trench 30cm (12in) wide. Then fill it with sharp sand. This severing makes the roots produce a new batch of feeding roots, growing into the sand. You're giving the shrub an intact, operational set of new roots for the moment it has moved.

The following year, get rid of one-third of the top growth by pruning the older stems. Then soak the soil around the rootball, giving it a drink, and spade down through the *outer* edge of that trench (not the inside edge because you'll simply spear through all the new root growth which is precisely what you want to keep) and haul out the plant, gently gently, lifting it onto a large, thick plastic sheet. Carry it to the new incredibly well-weeded site, having already dug its hole (twice the width of the rootball), and replant to the same depth as before. Mix organic matter with the excavated soil, which goes to the sides of the hole, not under the plant. Thump down the soil, getting rid of any air pockets, water and add a mulch so that the moisture doesn't quickly evaporate. Water in summer during dry spells. Easy.

Winter shrubs for scent, berries and flowers

There are plenty of good summer shrubs, but these are the ones you need. Given an average size garden, you only need four or five. How long the berries hang on depends on the birds. In alphabetical order . . .

Fig. 10. How to move a mature shrub.

Abeliophyllum distichum – a small, slow-growing shrub, 1.2m (4ft) high at most, with late winter white flowers on the bare stems giving a whiff of vanilla. A backing wall facing the sun, bouncing back the heat, is absolutely essential.

Buddleia auriculata – rarely gets a mention but it gives a good intake of sandalwood on warm, still days from autumn to early winter. Pure cream-white flowers. Being a South African native it needs shelter and good drainage.

Callicarpa bodinieri 'Profusion' – hundreds of tiny, shiny lilac balls on bare winter branches. For the rest of the year it's a bit of a no-no, so grow a summer annual up it.

Chimonanthus praecox – you'd never in a million years buy wintersweet if you saw it growing in midsummer. It's a right carthorse and takes five years to flower, but then the small yellow flowers break in midwinter on the bare branches giving a very spicy scent.

Christmas box (*Sarcococca*) – *S. confusa* and *S. hookeriana* have a very decent show of scented winter flowers followed by tiny black fruit. Both can be grown as low hedges.

Clematis cirrhosa 'Freckles' – evergreen with pink flowers and red speckling inside in late winter and good seedheads.

Coronilla valentina – chunky rounded evergreen with flashy yellow mid- and late-winter flowers, nicely scented, with more in summer; *C. v.* subsp. *glauca* has bluish-green leaves, and 'Variegata' has white edges.

Daphne odora 'Aureomarginata' – absolutely essential with an exquisite knockout scent whiffable 6m (20ft) away. Reliable evergreen flowering in late winter and early spring. Any trouble – and daphnes are notoriously tricky – then try the likes of the easy *D. tangutica*, with mid-spring flowers and more in summer, in another part of the garden. If you've got chalk, grow the slightly smaller *D. mezereum* for mid- and late-winter flowers. If you get totally hooked *D. bholua* 'Jacqueline Postill' flowers from Christmas to early spring, though 'Peter Smithers' and 'Penwood' have a better show of leaves after flowering. 'Jacqueline Postill' can actually look quite desperate, which is quite natural, so don't panic and start giving it extra gulps of water because you'll kill it. 'Spring Beauty' and 'Spring Herald' continue the show through the rest of the season. Provide moist, free-draining soil and a sunny sheltered position. Daphnes don't like battering winds. Grow them amongst deciduous shrubs to keep the roots shady and cool in summer. Also add a thick mulch. They hate extremes, so give them a drink in a drought. And don't let them bake or move them when established. Dig one up and you'll slice through the deep roots and it'll gradually, miserably die. I said they were tricky.

Decaisnea fargesii – a double whammy because this Chinese shrub has 90cm (3ft) long pinnate leaves – which doesn't mean you get one whacking great big leaf because a pinnate means divided into mini leaflets – and striking metallic-blue autumn fruit like a broad bean. Also 45cm (18in) long clusters of tiny yellow-green flowers in late spring. Not exactly winter but worth mentioning. Good rarity value because nobody seems to grow it.

Edgworthia chrysantha – pale yellow (red in the case of 'Red Dragon') scented flowers with silky hairs on bare winter branches.

Elaeagnus x *ebbingei* – not really winter, more autumn evenings when it has a fruity scent (like the related *E. macrophylla*) and silvery leaves.

Hamamelis x *intermedia* 'Pallida' and 'Jelena' – the Chinese witch hazels, with spidery leaves, flower on bare winter branches. If buying other witch hazels, do so in winter when you can check the strength of the scent. These are nicely fruity.

Ilex – see pages 66–7 for hollies. There's also *I. ketambensis* with 2.5cm (1in) long berries, the biggest for a holly, though you'll need to live in Indonesia or Sumatra.

Lonicera fragrantissima – *the* scented honeysuckle for winter, with bare winter branches and cream-white flowers followed by red berries. The buds appear before the last of the autumn leaves have dropped, and keep opening until the first of the spring foliage. Pick flowering branches and bring indoors.

Mahonia x *media* 'Lionel Fortescue' – plenty of packed, powerful arching stems getting 2.4 x 2.7m (8 x 9ft) high and wide and then, right in the gloom of winter, a yodelling explosion of sulphur yellow flowers. Spiky, dark green holly-like leaves. Semi-shade is best. After flowering prune some branches at waist and some at shoulder height and next year it'll flower at different levels. If left it gets tall and leggy, and you'll be craning your neck, straining to get a whiff. 'Charity' is a terrific alternative. For shape not scent try *M. lomariifolia* but it needs a warm, protective wall.

Pyracantha – even in a dismal patch of sad ground it'll slam out stiff stems and bright red or yellow berries. Train round windows, so you can watch the birds take the fruit, or up a wall making patterns.

Ribes laurifolium – flowering currant; evergreen for tying in against a wall with greenish-yellow clusters of flowers at the end of winter, then fruit turning from red to black.

Roses – for the biggest, fattest berries get *R.* 'Scabrosa', a great flowering bush, 1.5m (5ft) high, belting out crimson-pink flowers. *R. moyesii* 'Geranium' has flash red flowers and terrific hips (the show-offs term for a berry). *R. macrophylla* 'Master Hugh' has monsters like tiny chef's hats and, for more dangling out of trees you could go insane and grow *R. filipes* 'Kiftsgate' which hits 15m (50ft).

Rubus cockburnianus – a thicket of a deciduous shrub which looks like it has been sprayed white in winter. Makes a sharp contrast with the small, black, grass-like perennial *Ophiopogon planiscapus* 'Nigrescens'.

Viburnum – a four-way choice between the incredibly richly scented *V.* x *bodnantense*, *V.* x *burkwoodii*, *V. farreri* (and its cultivars, especially 'Candidissimum') and *V. grandiflorum* 'Snow White'. The first has clustered, tiny pinkish flowers up the bare winter stems, the second is semi-evergreen with white spring flowers, and the deciduous third has more white winter flowers. Buy all four and make sure they're in a sheltered place where that scent won't get blown away. Plant where they'll avoid winter frosts and a summer drought.

Also try a berrying cotoneaster (see page 66).

6

THE FLOWER GARDEN

Planting a border; what goes where?

(a) That's up to you but (b) make sure you've got colours, shapes and structures to make it snappy and fun in winter. Any loon can make a summer border, but one that's good all year . . . That takes TRIAL AND ERROR.

Do check that . . .

- If you've got a plant that's a one-season wonder (eg a peony), you plant something close that'll flower before or after so you don't get horrible great big gaps.

- You've got clusters of smart plants for each season.

- You buy smaller plants in threes or fives because one will get lost.

- You buy from specialist nurseries because they've got a far, far finer range of plants than a bog-standard, quick-turn around garden centre. And they know what they're talking about.

- You don't just have team photos with the tallest plants at the back and the shrimps at the front because, while potentially hugely impressive in stately homes, there's another look. You can also inject scatterings of varied shapes and sizes and see-through verticals (like fennel and *Verbena bonar-iensis*) making you peer round and through. Some plants stand out clearly, others get seen through a haze. Keep the garden varied.

- You leave room for larger plants to expand.

- Strong scents and the tactile are near the front.

- Big, boisterous plants are kept away from the restrained or they'll get swamped.

- Contrasting colours (with reds, yellows and blues) break out around the garden so that different areas keep grabbing the eye.

- You cultivate green as a colour with olive, apple, lime green, etc.

- You play with adjacent, different shapes. Keep creating surprises.

- The most exquisite colours aren't always packed tight together; put some with "feebler" colours. Their function is to make the good look Awesome.

- You cheat, copying/amending good arrangements from other gardens.

- You spray weedkiller on visiting snobs . . .

- While remaining magnificently snobbish.

Scent

There are so many scented plants it's bonkers to buy the non-whiffy kind. Make sure you grow them where they get full sun in a sheltered site where the scent can hang in the air. Most scented plants are climbers (see pages 73–6), shrubs (pages 82–6), annuals (pages 103–4) and bulbs (pages 105–13). Few are perennials. But first some Googled info.

1. The olfactory nerves go to a primitive part of the brain called the Limbic System which is associated with certain aspects of behaviour, memory and emotion. That's why smells make such an impact. The information then gets wired to the higher cortical regions for perception and interpretation.
2. We can smell from 4,000–10,000 different odours, and no two substances smell exactly alike.
3. As we get old our sense and taste declines. If you're 80 years old there's an 80 per cent chance that you'll have a major smell dysfunction, with men (as ever) doing worse than women. Right. Now the plants and some repeats.

Heady, powerful (shrubby) scents
Daphnes – a big whammy in spring. Since the weather can be awful, make sure they are in a prime sheltered sunny position (see page 84).

Hesperis matronalis – once you've got it growing it'll self-seed and generate large clusters of small white flowers with a sweet, early evening scent.

Jasminum officinale – it'll quickly whip up a drainpipe against a sunny wall; train the stems around open windows. Or let it burst through a hedge (see page 74).

Mexican orange blossom (*Choisya ternata*) – can be a freestanding evergreen shrub, but against a sunny wall at the back of a border it spreads and stretches and can easily grow 3.6m (12ft) wide by 2.4m (8ft) high. Fresh green leaves. Takes any amount of cutting back and shaping but only AFTER it has flowered. In a sheltered courtyard it blasts you with high-powered scents at the end of spring, with occasional smaller scatterings. Tear the leaves in two for the smell of black pepper. Thrives in hot, dry ground.

Mock orange (*Philadelphus*) – it's a toss up between the likes of 'Beauclerk' and 'Belle Etoile'. Big arching twiggy shrubs absolutely engulfed in early summer with papery white flowers wafting out bubblegum and Eau Sauvage.

Night-scented stock (*Matthiola bicornis*) – just buy a packet of seeds and scatter. Powerfully rich. Whenever you've a gap at the front of the flower bed, fill it with all you've got.

Rhododendron luteum – more a woodland plant, but it has bright yellow spring flowers with a scent that rides the warmth. And the leaves turn brash red in October.

Sweet peas (*Lathyrus*) – smell like a Crabtree & Evelyn talcum powder factory explosion (see page 76).

Get-your-nose-in scents
Brugmansia – tall, shrubby South American plants grown for their large flappy leaves, a good (25cm/10in) long, and long tubular flowers with a strong, sweet early evening scent. *B*. x *candida* 'Grand Marnier' is apricot and 'Knightii' white, as is *B. suaveolens*. Most spectacular when you strip off the lower shoots and force all the flowering growth high up, creating a standard with 1-3 legs. Grow outside in summer and then cut back, pot up and bring under cover or they'll rot in the wet. If they're getting too big, throw away the parent and use the pruned lengths as cuttings. They take very quickly on a windowsill.

According to Frohne and Pfander's standard German work on *Poisonous Plants*, the toxic seeds of the related *Datura stramonium* were a popular form of suicide in India. The leaves were also used by horse-dealers. They'd shove them up a moth-eaten old horse's bum so it'd prance around and they'd get a high price. The plants are also hallucinogenic. The same book refers to some boys who kept leaping into a pond looking for red-eyed dolphins.

Buddleias – if you're convinced that all the butterflies are dead, grow one of these and you'll find out. The zillions of clustered tiny flowers have a strong, sweet, lung-filling scent.

Cosmos atrosanguineus – deep plum-purple midsummer flowers that whiff of hot chocolate when the sun comes out. Grow in a pot and bring under cover over winter.

Heliotropium arborescens – in white, pinks, purple and violet, these shrubby plants, often grown as annuals because they don't live that long, make terrific front of border plants, or they can be grown en masse in small beds with feature plants erupting above. Or just grow one in a pot and keep by a sunny window for a mix of marzipan and vanilla. Can be tricky to keep over winter. Needs to be dry; just give the occasional sip.

Lilies – especially *L. regale,* but slugs can be a major nightmare. One day the short sturdy shoots are breaking through the soil, the next the tops have been demolished. No more until next year.

Magnolia grandiflora – a giant of a wall shrub (a free-standing tree in southern Europe, where it produces fruiting cones), needing a hot sunny wall in the UK. Huge shiny evergreen leaves and spectacularly large white flowers with a lemon scent. The best cultivars for the UK are 'Exmouth' and 'Goliath'.

Moroccan broom (*Cytisus battandieri*) – the tangy pong of a pineapple (and that's not hyperbole). Grow as a wall-trained tree for its yellow summer flowers. Quite happy in poor, dry soil.

Narcissi – ie short daffodils, especially the Jonquils. Grow them in pots on a windowsill where you can get your nose in. They deserve better than being goblin-height in the garden on a cold windy day.

Roses – they won't fling scent across a garden, but they can deliver a sweet kick when you get your nose in. See page 74.

Making a pot-pourri
Pick a wide range of flowers and leaves in early morning just as the sun has dried the dew. Dampness makes them deteriorate. To dry, place the petals, etc (minus discarded stems) on sheets of fine muslin on a wire cake rack in an airy, shady room. Alternatively hang in bunches from a ceiling beam. Note: don't dry in the oven because it invariably results in scorching. And dry the roses separately from the lavender, etc, as different plants dry at different speeds.

When dry and brittle put a mixed layer in a glass storage jar. Add a sprinkling of orris root powder – which is a vital fixative preserving all the scents – and continue building up in layers. Finally add drops of an oil, say rosemary or sandalwood. Then cover the jar with a tight lid, and store in a dark cupboard for 4–5 weeks, giving the occasional shake.

There's no fixed recipe. You select the ingredients. Try a mix of roses and scented geraniums with herbs like chamomile, lavender, lemon verbena, marjoram, and thyme, etc, mixed with dried citrus peel, spices, and myrrh.

Perfect pongers
Some plants are worth growing because they are so comically vile. The smell is stupendous. Those to try, avoid or imagine include . . .

Amorphophallus titanum, from Sumatra, is a gigantic erupting purple 'flower' which bursts vertically out the ground in three weeks with a gynormous phallic spike poking out. Grows 0.9–1.5m (3–5ft) high, and to attract pollinators double-quick it smells like hell and mimics the colour of rotting flesh. Also has a corm weighing 70 kilos (11 stone) and a pleated lip 2.4m (8ft) in circumference. What looks like the giant flower technically isn't a flower but a modified bract, and the phallic bit is a 1.8m (6ft) high tapering spadix. The real flowers are snucked out of sight at the base.

Rafflesia arnoldii is the world's most stupendous single flower. It's 90cm (3ft) wide, a magical jungle parasite which suddenly erupts out of its host (eg tropical vines). It's nearly always attached to the stem but I've heard reports it inhabits lianas. Like a parachute snagged in the tree canopy. What price that in your border, smelling of fried eggs and hippo.

Equally preposterous are *Orbea* (*Stapelia*) *variegata* (like a volley of fresh excrement), the Himalayan Voodoo lily (*Sauromatum venosum*), strongest a few hours after dawn (more excrement), *Dracunculus canariensis* from the Canary Islands (which apparently smells like semen), and the N. American *Aristolochia grandiflora* (fish).

And then there's *Dracunculus* (*Helicodiceros*) *muscivorus*. It's got a huge inflorescence (ie packed-together tiny flowers on a spike) like a mare's tail, has a decent mix of creams and pinks, and stinks incredibly goaty. In Majorca it's pollinated by big, powerful 18mm (½in) long flies which lay their eggs up body cavities (eg dead animals' ears and rectum), so again the plant mimics the smell and the colour to get pollinated. Inside the inflorescence are loads of tough bristles which the flies brush aside to get in and out, but the

UK flies are much too weedy and eventually they collapse and die. That's why it won't set fruit here, unless you pollinate with a paintbrush.

An easily grown stinky UK alternative is *Dracunculus vulgaris*. Nowhere near as stunning but it pongs like a Bulgarian loo and survives down to −5°C (23°F). It's got a mottled, snake-like stem, a shiny maroon spadix in early summer and grows about 90cm (3ft) high. It really is quite a beauty. You can also try *Ginkgo biloba* because the moment the fruit decomposes and gets squishy you get a blast of cheesy old knickers. (The nuts are used in Japanese and Chinese cookery.) And the N. American *Umbellularia californica* might well lead to a fistful of dispirin. The Victorians said it caused thumping-bad headaches.

Two viburnums to avoid are *V. foetidum* and *V. tinus*, especially the latter. It reeks of cats and fish, and flowers overwinter. And beware if you like the arums. *Arum nigrum* and *A. dioscoridis*; both are blackish-purple, about 30–40cm (12–16in) high, spring-flowering and real honkers. The inflorescence has minute flowers on a fleshy spadix and an upper sterile portion that's coated in a cocktail of chemicals. The flowers open in late afternoon and the spadix rapidly heats up, volatizing the chemicals. Amines emit the fishy smells, skatoles dung and butraldehyde vomit.

Not in the same league but perfectly good for spring are two foxy-smelling fritillaries, *F. pyrenaica* and *F. imperialis*. The pongiest autumn plants are *Biarum tenuifolium* (odious 'breath', like having a snog with an albatross) and *Arum pictum*, which is much more tender and needs winter-warmth indoors. And you can fill out any gaps with giant hogweed, stinking hellebores and stinkhorns (a fungus I'm afraid; either it strikes or not).

Large-leaved exotica

Great flapping leaves are fun, but they'll need sheltered areas because they get flayed in open, windy areas. And while they used to be banned from small gardens, designers have now decided that instead of packing a small space with tiny leaved plants to make it seem bigger – when you simply created a dolls' house effect – packing in thumping great big exotic plants gives (a) the sub-tropical look and (b) hides the sides so creating the impression, as you hack and thwack your way through, that you're inside a horticultural Tardis. Useful ingredients include . . .

Agave americana – a giant of a spiky succulent which grows like a weed in southern Europe, packed together on sunny slopes. Usually a conservatory plant, big mature ones should be able to survive outdoors in mild inner cities or the far south-west, but it needs an incredibly stony, gritty south-facing bank so that the rain sluices straight through the ground. Or grow one in a pot. Can eventually exceed 1.2m (4ft) high and wide. The tips are viciously sharp. If that's a problem, cut them off or ram ping pong balls on the end.

Banana (*Musa basjoo*) – the largest plant on earth without a woody stem. You've got to be dedicated but you will get 1.8m (6ft) long arching leaf blades. A tropical plant for the UK. Give the roots plenty of muck and water well, especially in dry weather, and feed. After fruiting, and yes it will produce a cluster of bananas under glass, the stem dies but there's new replacement growth from low down. It is a suckering peren-nial, and you might well need to remove that new growth if you haven't got room for it. To keep it over winter, either pot up and wheel into a frost-free conservatory or cut off the main leaves after they have been frosted and then slide a cage of chicken wire/chimney pot liners around the stem, and pack it with straw. Not pretty but effective. By preserving the stem it should easily get 4m (12ft) high, even reaching 6m (20ft).

Remove the protection the following spring when the temperate is stuck above 10°C (50°F) and new growth will emerge from the top. Even if you forget, leaving it out in the frost, it should still regrow from the bottom.

Bear's breeches (*Acanthus mollis*) – forget the flowers (well I hate them) but those glossy dark green leaves (*mollis* is Latin for soft) can get 90cm (3ft) long, but slug attacks are a nightmare.

Caster oil plant (*Ricinus communis*) – grown as an annual, it belts up to 1.8m (6ft) tall with splayed leaves about 30cm (12in) long. Large, luxuriant, sub-tropical.

Chinese rhubarb (*Rheum palmatum*) – perennial with huge, coarse leaves getting up to 90cm (3ft) long.

Colocasia esculenta 'Fontanesii' – 82cm (32in) high with shiny black stems and whopping green arrow-like leaves, 40 x 25cm (16 x 10in). If you want the all-black version, go for 'Black Magic'. Likes semi-shady, rich moist ground. Treat like a dahlia, and dig up in autumn, keeping the tubers dryish in a frost-free place over winter.

Dasylirion acrotrichum – spectacularly amazing and dangerous, it makes a great erupting ball of bendy spear-like leaves, which you can't help flicking to send ripples all over the plant, but accidentally fall into one and you'd have a stomach like a colander. Very slow growing, eventually getting 1.5m (5ft) high and wide. Good in mild coastal gardens in fast-draining ground with plenty of added grit, or pots when it'll need regular summer watering. With luck you'll eventually get a 3m (10ft) plus high flower spike.

Echium pininana – a biennial from the Canaries, growing the first year and flowering and dying the second, when it scatters its seed and creates great thickets. The 3m (10ft) high flower spikes are the big attraction, but the rosettes of long leaves are hugely exotic. See page 26.

Fatsia japonica – usually grown in shady corners, it quickly fills a large space getting 2.2m (7ft) high and wide with glossy dark green leaves getting 30cm (12in) long and more. A hungry outdoor plant.

Fig – has gynormous hand-size leaves. You'll also get a good crop outside in the UK if you choose the reliable 'Brown Turkey' or 'Brunswick'. As a free-standing specimen figs make chunky, shrubby trees, 3m (10ft) high and wide. To keep them at a manageable size, lock up their roots in a barrel with John Innes No. 3 or plant it against a south-facing house wall in a pit 60cm (2ft) wide and deep. Insert paving slabs vertically against the four pit walls, and line the bottom with rubble. This improves the drainage but won't stop the roots eventually escaping.

To get a good crop with branches nicely paced out against the baking hot brickwork, nip back the main stem in spring just above two strong shoots. This forces them to grow out to the side, and keep them at 40 degrees to the horizontal by tying them to long canes, which in turn are tied to a horizontal system of wall wires. Nip these two branches back to keep them at 45cm (18in) long. See Fig. 11 overleaf.

The following spring, reduce all the new growth breaking from these two side branches to half their length, and tie each one of these new lengths to its own cane to guarantee a well-spaced fan shape with every branch getting plenty of sun. The following winter, do the same, and so on.

Water well in the early years while the roots are still locked up in the pit, and give a tomato feed in early summer. Two crops will then be produced. The fruit (a fig isn't actually a fruit, it's an inside-out conglomeration of flowers; cut one open and you'll see the scores of miniscule flowers) emerges as a tiny green embryonic globe like a hard pea at the end of summer. Leave

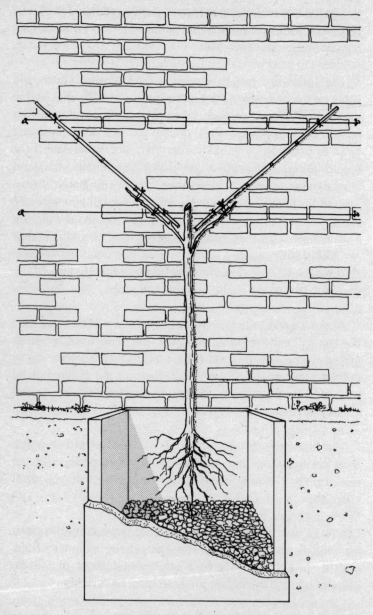

Fig. 11. How to prune a fig.

this on the tree to develop next spring and gradually fatten. The second crop appears in midsummer but won't have time to ripen outside and needs to be shaken off in autumn. Don't leave it on or the small peas will take longer to grow and ripen.

The following spring remove the tip of the branch, but leave on the pea, to generate more fruiting side shoots. And in midsummer nip them back when they have developed four leaves. Done properly, you'll double the size of the crop and get it to harvest two weeks earlier than otherwise. And if the whole thing, however it is grown, eventually becomes horribly congested, or you get long, bare unproductive stems, just cut back and they'll quickly reshoot though you will lose that year's crop. Just one word of warning. When cutting back branches or removing autumn figs, beware the sap. It's an incredibly sticky gloopy glue, so don't get it on your clothes. And wear kitchen gloves because (a) it's a devil to get off and (b) some people are highly allergic to it.

Gunnera manicata – one for the bog garden (see page 157) but you will need plenty of room for its high-powered summer growth when it gets 2.5m (8ft) high and even wider. Grow enough plants and you'll create a shady length of jungle, and you can comfortably stand upright beneath the canopy of chunky, leathery leaves.

Indian bean tree (*Catalpa bignonioides*) – fast-growing tree with 25cm (10in) long leaves and long thin pods, after the flowers, up to 40cm (16in) long. Good choice if you need quick shade.

Loquat (*Eriobotrya japonica*) – another shrub-cum-evergreen tree which needs rich clay soil and regular summer drinks with a spring feed to give a really good show of leaves. They're up to 30cm (12in) long, arching and crinkly.

Magnolia macrophylla – the magnolia for large leaves; they're up to 60cm (2ft) in the UK but on the flimsy side. It's best grown in North America where it flowers prolifically producing even bigger whoppers, up to 45cm (18in) wide, than *M. grandiflora*'s flowers. *M. tripetala* has leaves over 30cm (12in) long.

Palms – *Chamaerops humilis* is a slow-growing, reasonably hardy Mediterranean with a stiff mop of 60cm (2ft) long splayed leaves. Unlikely to exceed 1.2m (4ft) high and wide after two decades. The Chusan palm (*Trachycarpus fortunei*) is the hardiest palm in the world, and has a batch of splayed, fan-like leaves, about 60cm (2ft) long, arrayed around the shaggy trunk. In Christine Shaw's book *Architectural Plants* she gives a very good way of stripping off this hairy covering. Use a sharp bread knife to slice off the coat and expose the whitish bark beneath.

Paulownia tomentosa – don't just plant and go because it needs coppicing, cutting right down to the ground in spring which channels all its energy into a flagpole stem with just a few high-up, 60cm (2ft) wide leaves. You won't get any flowers but so what?

Rhododendron sinogrande – a shrub-cum-tree, it has shiny dark green leaves, initially silvered, which might exceed 60cm (2ft) long and 25cm (10in) wide. They're the largest of any rhodo with a strong show of large pale yellowish-white flowers. The plant hunter Frank Kingdon Ward described how "The great spear-headed buds burst in July, and even in August one can pick out the tree a few miles away by the plumes of silver foliage shooting up from ruby-red tubes." Decent alternatives, but not in the same league, are *R. falconeri* with 35cm (14in) long leaves and *R. rex* at 45cm (18in) at best.

Rice paper plant (*Tetrapanax papyrifera*) – invariably multi-stemmed evergreen shrub/small tree which might get 5m (15ft) high, with splayed leaves from 30–50cm (12–20in) wide. Not totally hardy but will regenerate from low down after a fierce winter. If it gets too bare and leggy, cut it right back in spring to force out new thicker growth.

And finally, *Rosa sericea* f. *pteracantha*. It hasn't got large leaves but has got translucent winged red thorns on young shoots, like the cresting on a tropical lizard.

Grasses

The crucial point about grasses is that they can make substantial blocks of spurting, arching growth with elegant airy panicles high above, and can be left over winter adding shape and substance before being cut back at the end of winter, before the new growth appears. Don't hack that off. Grasses break up borders, adding plenty of substance, and can also be grown in a ring around a tree or against the edge of an artificial pond, hiding the sides, dangling over the water. The choice is vast, and the only way to buy is to visit a specialist nursery. Here are the top contenders.

You'd have to be sozzled to ignore *Stipa gigantea* (a great grass *and* a great plant) which tops 2m (6ft) high. In early summer there's a head-high burst of golden spikelets, like a flowering oat, well above the foliage, and to get the best effect it needs to be lit by the evening sun against a dark background, eg a beech hedge. The spikelets gradually fade to straw and should be left on over winter, if children haven't grabbed them as swords. 'Gold Fontaene' has slightly larger flowers. Don't confuse with the mini *Stipa tenuissima,* a terrific 60cm (2ft) high cluster of fine wiry, grass-like leaves which are extremely responsive to the wind. One by itself is hopeless. You need large numbers to pack a small bed with feature plants erupting above. Poor, free-draining ground is essential where it should self-seed. Don't cavalierly throw them out because they are short-lived and you will need more. If the soil is too rich the growth flops.

Molinia caerulea subsp. *arundinacea* is another head-high biggy, possibly hitting 1.8m (6ft), making a strong block of growth with a late summer burst of tall thin stems topped by tiny flowers. The leaves go yellow then orange and red in autumn. 'Karl Foerster' is still a top choice, and if you need a tall, narrowly stiffly upright plant go for 'Skyracer'. In autumn it glows fierce sugary-orange. The whole thing. Electric, alive and luminous. If you can't get it, apparently 'Zuneigung' is even better. A porcupine on fire. *Miscanthus sinensis* 'Gracillimus' keeps the show going (it has been popular for over 100 years, initially in Japan) by flowering late, at the start of autumn. The height – 2.2m (7ft) – is three times the width. Buy on sight because there's lots of variation. Go for a new modern hybrid because they flower in midsummer, not (unreliably) in the autumn. *Calamagrostis* x *acutiflora* 'Karl Foerster' (his name keeps cropping up because he was a famous grassophile-nurseryman-breeder) is slightly shorter at 2m (6½ft) and is equally useful because it makes another tight, vertical clump with wind-swished swaying panicles.

Deschampsia cespitosa is shorter and more delicate, a rich green cluster with a spectacular head of silver-green plumes all summer, turning autumn-russet, and there's no excuse for not growing it, especially in semi-shade, because it's the ultimate grow-anywhere grass at 90cm (3ft) high. When you need extra supplies, just dig up a mature plant and divide it into several sections. *D. flexuosa* is slightly shorter, and for the best bluish grass, at 30cm (1ft) high, get the evergreen *Festuca glauca* 'Elijah Blue'. When its centre starts becoming rather feeble, eventually petering out, and it will, just dig it up, chuck out the old inner part and replant the more productive outer sections. There are other forms with varying degrees of blueness. All like light soil with excellent drainage. If you cut back the plants in spring and summer you'll get a batch of new growth and that colour.

If you want something even taller, then the giant reed (*Arundo donax*) – so tall everyone thinks it's a bamboo – is the top choice. At 4.2m (14ft), and it grows that each summer from scratch, it needs a special position. But what are you going to grow it with? Other large-leaved plants (see page 95) or go for shock value by letting it rip where unexpected. It's surprisingly easy to restrain if it starts spreading because you can just slice down through the soft underground growth, but don't even think about digging up an old clump and dividing it.

And finally two to grow round the apple trees. *Briza media* makes small annual clumps, getting 60cm (2ft) high with summer spikelets like "puffy oats", to quote *the* grass expert Rick Darke. They shake, rattle and roll in the wind. *Hordeum jubatum* is a 23cm (9in) high waft of silvery tassles with a pinkish/reddish tint in the panicles. It doesn't live long but with luck self-seeds everywhere. In parts of America it's a noxious weed. Fringing paths or to the front of a border it beats annuals hands down.

After that, check out the panicums (especially *P. virgatum*) and pennisetums (*P. alopecuroides* 'Hameln') and specialist nurseries which keep introducing new plants, and best of all *The Encyclopedia of Grasses for Livable Landscapes* (Timber Press) by Mr. Darke. The only thing lacking is photographs of grasses in autumn, trampolining with spiders' webs. And *Phaenosperma globosa*, an Asian grass with bamboo-like leaves at ground level and 1.2m (4ft) long stems topped by large white seeds, firing off in all directions. Angle through deep dark luscious red roses.

Annuals and biennials
Whenever I see one of those happy chimps presenting a TV gardening programme, they're in high gushing mode marking out a patch for different coloured annuals while I'm screaming "Don't" because whenever I try growing annuals everything gets gobbled by wood pigeons (look outside at 5am and they're swaggering around the garden smörgåsbording), slugs (goose-

stepping in from the field next door) and mice. So if you want my advice, don't do it. Unless you sow them indoors in pots and wait until they're quite big and then plant them out.

That said, grow *Amaranthus caudatus*, Californian poppies (*Eschscholzia californica*), Caster oil plant (*Ricinus communis*), *Cerinthe major* var. *purpurascens*, *Cleome spinosa*, *Cobaea scandens*, *Colocasia esculenta* 'Black Magic', cone flowers (*Rudbeckia*), cosmos, foxgloves (*Digitalis*), gazanias, hollyhocks (*Alcea*), larkspur (*Delphinium*), morning glory (*Ipomoea*), night-scented stock (*Matthiola bicornis*), petunias, sweet peas (*Lathyrus*), sweet rocket (*Hesperis*), tobacco plants (*Nicotiana sylvestris*), *Verbena bonarensis* and best of all avenues of sunflowers (*Helianthus*) leading to your moat and manor house, and you'll be ecstatic.

Perennials

They shoot up in spring, flower in summer, die back in autumn. On and on. Year after year. Except some are quite short-lived. If you've only got perennials in a border it'll be a slab of mud for five months, so make sure you've got plenty of all-year shrubs and grasses or you could get Highly Depressed. If they start underperforming after several years, they're getting clapped out and need dividing. This eliminates the old, exhausted inner portions and keeps the livelier outer sections. There's a choice of over 5,000 which I've insanely narrowed down to 12. (Well you have a go.)

1. *Anemone* x *hybrida* 'Königin Charlotte'
2. *Aquilegia* – any from the State Series
3. *Eremurus robustus*
4. Himalayan blue poppy (*Meconopsis betonicifolia*)
5. *Knautia macedonica*
6. *Lobelia cardinalis*
7. *Paeonia mlokosewitschii*
8. Red-hot poker *(Kniphofia uvaria* 'Nobilis')
9. *Salvia patens*

10. *Stipa gigantea*
11. *Viola* 'Bowles Black' and, for gobbets of God's spectacular blood, which have meteored down to earth, the totally indispensable . . .
12. Dahlias. They grow from multiplying fattening tubers turning into a great big lump of packed-together small potatoes and can need quite a bit of care. Colours range from the pink of a baby's eyelid to rich purple ('Hillcrest Royal'), yellows, whites and bicolours (with the likes of yellow and red). Unless you've got really open, sluicing free-draining ground and live in a mild area they need digging up after they have been frosted or the tubers rot and go gooey in the British winter wet. (If you can leave them in the soil, put a hefty pile of protective winter mulch on top.) Then cut off the top growth, let them dry and give them a dose of fungicide (horticultural, life-saving "talcum powder" which will stop them rotting).

Keep them in a tray in a garage over winter in sawdust or polystyrene chips, giving them an occasional spray with water to stop them completely drying out. Next spring pot them up and the extra warmth will generate lots of new shoots. Plant them out at the start of summer, by which time the slugs should have found easier, softer pickings (like those lilies). Four weeks later nip out the main stem to encourage plenty of flowering side-growth, and to stop the main stem becoming the dominant shoot.

Bulbs

New gardeners seem to think bulbs have a huge sign over them screaming "Go Away, Danger, Impossibly Hard to Grow." Which is crazy. You just dig a hole and drop them in. And when I say the right way up, you try distinguishing head from arse when holding a cyclamen or an anemone. So lie the puzzlers on their sides. Let them sort it out. The shoots will soon head for the light.

'Bulbs', of course, don't just mean bulbs. They mean corms, rhizomes, tubers, and fleshy rooted plants though you don't want to get bogged down in detail. They're all underground/near-surface flower bombs waiting to ignite. They range from tiny, coconut blobs to what look like flattened, frazzled cowpats, with no indication what might happen. Some shoot up 20 times the height of the bulb. That is like getting a hill to erupt out of an African elephant, and in just a matter of weeks.

The point about bulbs is that they are great survivors. In Namaqualand, south-west of the Kalahari Desert, it gets 40°C (104°F) but get a spade and dig, and there are underground shelves with bulbs and corms, freesias and amaryllis, layer on layer, waiting for it to rain. Then voooomph. Three weeks of flowery mayhem. One definition is that bulbs shoot up, perform when the conditions are right, then become a lumpen thing again, dormant until next year, living on stored-up energy. Some, like the giant lily (*Cardiocrinum giganteum*), take three or four years to rev up, a kind of quivering, fattening presence, before it whacks up 1.8m (6ft) high stems (capable of hitting 4m/13ft), each with about 20 richly scented flowers, whereupon it goes phutt and dies, leaving offsets (baby bulbs), and then they repeat the cycle.

Planting

So where and how to plant them? First, not where you risk digging them up, spearing them with a wonderful splunk. And that happens. Marking the area with stones or sticks sounds clever but they *always* vanish. Planting them around shrubs, where you will not do any digging, is more sensible. Second, you can naturalize bulbs (eg letting the likes of crocuses multiply at will) in grass, but note you'll be stuck with long grass for a few weeks. If you mow and slash off the bulbs' foliage with it, after flowering but before they have died down, you will get pathetic flowers next year or even none; try it again and the bulbs die. You have got to leave bulbs' foliage on the plants – and that applies to all bulbs – no matter how tatty it looks, to store energy for next year's show.

Third, you can segregate bulbs and give them special beds or parts of beds, often the hottest, driest part of the garden where they can bake in summer, with snappy winter drainage. Or grow them at the front of a border or under trees for winter flowering, or in rockeries if they're small and fussy, needing quick drainage, or in containers sunk in water over summer (eg *Iris ensata*). They have got to be tricked into thinking they are in Azerbaijan or Turkey or wherever they come from. And fourth, if you want to try really tricky bulbs, buy an alpine house, a kind of horticultural isolation unit, a well-ventilated glasshouse which excludes the winter wet. The cold and dryness isn't a problem, it's the British mud and rain which kills them. Alpine houses are expensive; a converted glasshouse is cheaper, but note it'll need to have at least 20 per cent of the side panels replaced by ventilator openings.

When buying bulbs only buy large, firm bulbs and make holes in the ground using a trowel or special bulb planter. It's just like an apple corer and pulls plugs of soil straight out of the ground. The holes should be two to three times the depth of the bulb, but keep the bulb nearer the soil surface when the ground is heavy and plant them deeper when the soil is light and free draining. Prong up the ground at the bottom of the hole with a kitchen fork, plant and infill. When naturalizing, gently lob the bulbs on the ground and plant them where they land to give a fairly natural spread. Either plant them individually in the turf and put the grass lids back on top afterwards or slice round three sides of an imaginary square with a spade, roll back the turf, loosen the soil (if necessary), and then make the individual holes.

Feeding

You don't need to feed bulbs on planting because they've got their own energy supplies. What they might need is a power boost after flowering, before the leaves fade and they become dormant, when they're building up their energy supplies for next year (but note that some, like colchicums, actually flower before the leaves appear). A balanced fertilizer is fine.

Dividing

The ideal is a great block of colour but sometimes the bulbs procreate so vigorously that they need breaking up into smaller clumps. They get 'factory chicken-itis'. If you see the clumps getting very congested and the flowering rather feeble you know what to do; dig them up when they have finished flowering, and the leaves are fading, and replant with wider gaps. Snowdrops and aconites are certainly best divided *immediately* after flowering while they are still leafy (called "in-the-green").

The big three for late winter–spring

Daffodils first. There are about 1,700 kinds on the market with names like 'Frou-frou', 'Hoopoe', and 'Ufo'. The colour range is wide; apricot, lemon, orange, pink, white, and yellow. Flower shapes vary; there are 11 botanical groups, and a twelfth for the miscellaneous. *Narcissus triandrus* looks like a fuchsia with tightly pulled back petals and 'Broadway Star' like a zany lollipop. Heights range from the tiny, 10cm (4in) high delicate little North African *N. watieri* to the knee-high *N.* 'Stratosphere', at 65cm (26in). And they can be grown in different ways. In drifts in a grassy area, or in pots in the case of the dwarfs in a cold greenhouse where you can clearly see them. The rich, powerfully scented kind, like the Tazettas (check your choice; some get killed by the frost) and jonquils, both with several small flowers per stem, are also best in pots so that you can easily smell them. If going outside, they need a south-facing border in a mild region, backed by a sheltering wall, where the Tazettas can bake over summer.

When planting they need at least 15cm (6in) of soil above them because in mid- and late spring, if it hasn't rained, the topsoil quickly dries. Below that level the bulbs can fatten and drink all they want. Well-drained ground is also essential, and fine grass is better than choking, vigorous growth. And on poor soils sprinkle an all-purpose feed after flowering, before the foliage dies. Give the bulbs a chance.

To see how tulips should be grown, visit Monet's scrunched-in colour-booming garden at Giverny, north of Paris. He knew about blocks of colour. "Enormous fields in full bloom" he drooled, describing the Dutch tulip fields, "enough to drive a poor painter crazy."

Whatever hues you want, tulips have it: the juicy, brash, delicate and sharp. Flowering is generally mid- and late spring. They take a bit of care. Most bulbs need digging up after flowering and storing in a mouse-proof shoe box in a cool, dry place until re-planting in late autumn or early winter. Or Christmas if you forget. But do not re-plant them too early or they shoot up in the warmth and then get zapped by the winter frost. If left in the ground all year they might well rot and deteriorate, but you can try it. With luck they can last 30 years. The Greigii and Kaufmanniana hybrids are sturdy survivors.

The pick of the bunch include the amazingly elegant 'White Triumphator', with one white goblet on a 60cm (24in) high stem; beautiful with pink 'Angélique' standing over blue forget-me-nots. In fact any bright tulips like the yellow 'West Point' look sensational amongst forget-me-nots. 'Burgundy' is purple, 'Maytime' reddish-violet, 'China Pink' clear pink and 'Shirley' white with carmine. 'Queen of Night' is near black. The Parrot tulips are more Groucho Marx than Audrey Hepburn, with crimped, ragged petals and often a hodge-podge of colours. 'Estella Rijnveld' looks like an explosion of raspberries and white paint, and 'Flaming Parrot' shrieks yellow and crimson. Fast drainage is essential; also quickly remove the old petals and foliage the second they have died down to avoid an attack of tulip fire. And beware squirrels.

Now the irises. The bigger ones flower in summer, so for spring stick to the Reticulatas (like the reddish-purple

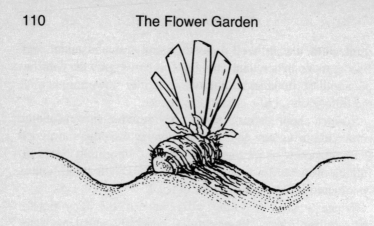

Fig. 12. How to plant irises.

'J.S. Dijit'). They're foolproof and small, barely getting above ankle height. And the Bearded kind (you'll have to look hard to see the 'beard'; it's just a small group of fluffy hairs on the falls or outer petals which, in the wild, may attract pollinating insects) have a shapely fan of upright, strap-shaped leaves but coming from desert regions of Israel and Iran, etc, they need really free-draining ground which isn't soaking wet for long winter spells and plant them right on top of the soil. The colour range is huge, and many have two or more colours.

Other spring bulbs include:

Anemone blanda – small clumps with a strong show of violet, blue, pink, magenta or white flowers. *A. coronaria* is in red, blue or white.

Bluebells (*Hyacinthoides*) – go for the swashbuckling Spanish bluebell (*Hyacinthoides hispanica*) in blue, pink or white with more presence than the English kind though without the scent, but do not put them in a border because you will *not* get them out. They spread and burrow, some 60cm (24in) down.

Crocuses – especially *C. tommasinianus,* 10cm (4in) high;

procreates like billy-o; it invades, expands and takes over. Good in open stretches of grass. Also try *C. chrysanthus* 'Ladykiller' in purple and white.

Fritillaria – striking spring to early summer flowers. Some make imposing eye-catchers (*F. imperialis*), others are good naturalizers (*F. meleagris*). Colours range from plum to orange to white; some bi-coloured (*F. michailovskyi*), others chequered (*F. latifolia*).

Hyacinths (*Hyacinthus orientalis*) – richly scented, with 50-odd names to choose from in reds, pinks, yellows, lilacs and blues. Many are indistinguishable but 'Queen of Violets' is rich and vivid, and 'Distinction' looks like it has just had sex with a beetroot.

Extra essentials: *Arisaema griffithii* (good for Gothic gardens because of the weird, veined, snake-like inflorescence), *Arisarum proboscideum*, *Arum dioscoridis* and *A. italicum*, *Chionodoxa*, the stinky *Dracunculus vulgaris* (see page 94), *Eranthis, Erythronium, Muscari, Ornithogalum nutans* and snowflakes (*Leucojum aestivum*).

The summer bulbs
Not as many but they include some of the best – the alliums, gladioli and irises, then the lilies, the amazing *Cardiocrinum giganteum*, crocosmias and eucomis.

The early summer, big-headed (called 'drumstick') alliums, like 'Purple Sensation', have a galactic star-burst of tiny flowers, with *Allium schubertii*'s purple head being 45cm (18in) wide, but others aren't such whoppers. Grow them in drifts and flanking paths. The easiest (and boldest) gladioli is *Gladiolus communis* subsp. *byzantinus* because it doesn't, like other gladioli, come from South Africa and need such free-draining ground. It makes a thumping reddish-purple clump in early summer. And the summer irises tend to be the Beardless

kind, with *I. ensata* and *I. laevigata* for the edge of a pond and
the *versicolor*s for the border. There are millions of hybrids to
choose from.

The midsummer lilies can be total stunners, especially the
scented kind like *L. regale*. To get a long lily season, kick off
with the Asiatic hybrids which open before midsummer, with
the Oriental types for late summer. And get a specialist
catalogue. The one big problem is that the emerging shoots,
the thick, fleshy poles, are smoked salmon for slugs and once
a shoot is chomped through, that's it for the year. That's why
many grow lilies in large pots filled with John Innes No. 2 and
wait until they're on the verge of flowering before standing
them out. And if you think they're impressive, wait until you
try *Cardiocrinum giganteum*. It blasts up a sturdy flower stem
with white lily-like flowers and a rich, lung-filling scent, with
huge 40cm (16in) long leaves at the base. Make sure it gets
rich, shady, slightly acid ground which doesn't dry out (or get
swamped) in summer.

Crocosmias aren't individual eye-catchers but 15 or more
in a group give arching apple green leafy growth and, in the
case of 'Lucifer', blasts of hothouse reds. For late summer
and early autumn you need eucomis. Ignore the tall kind,
like the 90cm (3ft) high *Eucomis comosa* 'Sparkling
Burgundy' because it sounds terrific but the flower spike
promptly flops and looks daft when tied to a stake, so go
for the quirkily bizarre *E. bicolor*, a perfectly sturdy 45cm
(18in). The purple-edged pale green flowers are packed
around the stem which is splashed with purple 'measles' and,
best of all, it gets a tufty crown of fleshy leaves-cum-petals.
Being South African, it demands open, quick-draining soil
that promptly warms up in spring, with 24/7 sunbathing all
summer at the foot of a sheltering wall. Pile on a hefty mulch
over winter, and don't feed in spring or that flower spike
will rocket up and go kaput.

Other essentials: *Calochortus venustus* (best in a pot),
Crinum x *powellii* 'Album', *Dierama pulcherrimum*, *Gloriosa*

superba, *Hymenocallis* x *festalis*, Iris 'Bumblebee Deelite', 'Shirley Pope' and *I. delavayi*, and *Zantedeschia*.

Autumn–-late winter bulbs
The three top bulbs are the cyclamen, snowdrop and more irises. *Cyclamen coum* gives hundreds of tiny roundish leaves, like discs on the ground, dark shiny green; some are silvery patterned, some nearly silver all over. And the flower stems stick straight up, with petals from white to pink to purple. Imagine the sun on that. The Pewter and Silver groups also give very good silver markings; 'Tilebarn Elizabeth' is bi-coloured, dark and pale pink. Plant them round the base of a tree in semi-shade, in rich soil with plenty of leafmould. You can bump up the December–March display with quick-spreading, autumn-flowering *C. hederifolium*. Note that the florist's scented *C. persicum* is too tender to grow outside. Grow it indoors in pots, the cooler the room the better. Anything above 10°C (50°F) and they can't hack it.

Snowdrops (*Galanthus*) are easily grown, and make good naturalizers. The white flowers are usually marked green, and open from late winter. There are scores of different names with the subtlest of miniscule differences. And the blue *Iris histrioides* thrives in the open ground, making decent clumps of deep blue, surviving frosts and blizzards.

Other essentials: *Colchicum autumnale*, *Crocus banaticus* and *C. kotschyanus*, and *Nerine bowdenii*.

Flower arranging and water lilies
If you thought that flower arranging meant jamming twigs at the back of a pot, daisies at the front, with a mini herbaceous border between. No. Here are the Idiot's 10 Steps to Success.

1. Take cuttings in the evening, then keep fresh in a bucket of water until morning.
2. Bash the stems with a hammer because this maximizes the area taking up water.

3. Choose a theme.
4. Fix the cut flowers in place using a pre-soaked Oasis-type block.
5. Start with the tallest stem, setting it absolutely vertically and slightly off-centre or you'll end up with a stiff, symmetrical look. Then create a light, fan-shaped background, slightly lower than the main stem.
6. Add a highly distinctive central focal point using a flower with a face, among an uneven number of flowers. Their colour will dominate. Some shapes (eg ivy) need to hang over the edge.
7. Check that... all stems curve to the focal point.
8. . . . each individual flower is clearly seen.
9. . . . all stems are well below the water line.
10. And fill the vase to the top, only refilling to top up.

You can also use water lilies as cut flowers. What puts many people off is that they close at night, when you want them displayed on the dinner table, but they won't if . . .

1. You use waterlilies which hold their flowers above the water; they mustn't sit on it. Cut them in early morning, leaving a long stem, and immediately put in a bucket of cold water to avoid wilting.
2. Hold the flowers upside down and drip molten wax from an ordinary household candle on the back of the base of the petals, so that the "hinge" where they close is locked solid.
3. Add to a display or, far better, float in a shallow tray of water on the dining room table.

Poisonous plants

Provided you're not bonkers and go round eating wisteria there's no problem but it's worth knowing what's out there. Especially if you've got children, dogs and grannies.

We've got about 1,500 native plants in the UK, and *c*. 150 are poisonous. They divide into three main categories: the potentially lethally toxic, the phototoxics (touch the foliage under ultra-violet sunlight and you'll get blisters the size of a squash ball), and the allergy-inducing plants or irritants.

Yew is one of the worst potential killers, corpsing humans, cows (kaput in six hours) and bulls. All parts are toxic if eaten, except for the fleshy fruit. My vet said he'd once had to dash down to Somerset where six cows had eaten a yew hedge. They died of internal haemorrhaging. Eyes as big as omelettes.

Hemlock water dropwort recently killed someone in just a few hours. He ate the tuber, packed with convulsant poison, having confused its fine feathery leaves with celery. And a family picking blackberries picked the shiny black berries of deadly nightshade (*Atropa bella-donna*). They cooked it in a pie and were ambulanced to intensive care, flushed faces, dry mouths, clattering hearts and dilated pupils (they recovered). Both plants are occasionally used by suicides.

While deadly nightshade hogs the headlines (2–5 berries can kill a child), it has got two nasty little-known relatives. Woody nightshade (*Solanum dulcamara*) with shiny red berries, though you'd need about 200 of the green unripe ones for a fatality, while black nightshade (*S. nigrum*) has surprisingly different toxicity levels, in different situations, rendering it harmless or toxic. You can't say precisely what berry dose is going to be lethal because, like all poisonous plants, toxicity varies with the plant, health, site, soil, climate, season, etc, and with the body's ability to absorb and detoxify.

Hellebores used to cause plenty of trouble, before everyone caught on. Discarded leaves can kill grazing animals and constant handling gives blisters. In Brian Mathew's excellent book on hellebores he cites a sickly nineteenth-century dissection; two people had gulped down a decoction of hellebore root in cider; sixteen hours later "the lungs were gorged with blood; the mucous membrane of the stomach was . . . a blackish-brown colour, and reduced almost to a gangrenous state." All that from a Christmas rose.

Florists recently got in a bit of a tizz about monkshood (*Aconitum*), which is one of the most poisonous plants in the UK (extracts of the related Indian *A. ferox* make a first-rate poison arrow). Eat a big plant for breakfast and you'll start to tingle and sweat, get thirsty and cold, vomit, scream, be paralyzed and die, probably conscious to the end. Laburnum is another nasty, especially if you're a hungry pooch. Gnaw at a branch and gulp down some pods and it'll be dead in 30 minutes. (Did you know pigs can die after eating fresh tomato shoots? They're high in tomatine, related to the poisonous green tissue you get in bad potatoes.)

Survive that little lot and you could still end up looking like ET's wrinkly granny, depending on how sensitive your skin is. Giant hogweed (*Heracleum mantegazzianum*) – 2.1m (7ft) high, which was brought to Europe in the 1890s because it was reckoned a stately plant – and fat hen (*Chenopodium album*) are a couple of nasties. Get their juice on the skin in sunlight and the flesh burns and badly blisters. You might even get a (permanent) dark brown scar. The classic case is schoolboys using hogweed stems for a peashooter. (One way to keep them quiet.) You're not even safe indoors. There's a vicious little primula (*P. obconica*), whose hairs are tipped with a chemical which causes a dermatitis-type reaction. And don't touch the likes of American poison ivy (*Toxicodendron radicans*) or *T. rydbergii,* or the poisonous oaks (*T. diversiloba* or *T. toxicarium)* because they'll give a hell of a nasty rash, or confuse daffodil bulbs with onions (which happens) in which case you'll explode at either end with spectacular diarrhoea and vomiting.

So how come some plants can do this? Botanists used to think that some toxins were the waste products of a plant's metabolism; now they stress they're survival tactics against herbivorous insects and grazing animals. Some toxins also ensure the fruit tastes bitter until it's ripe, when it's palatable and can be widely dispersed in birds' faeces.

The National Poisons Unit at Guy's Hospital, London, used

to get about 6,000 plant-related calls a year, a fair number concerning toddlers who'd eaten berries instead of sweets. (Provided a doctor is contacted immediately, and shown a piece of the plant, it's unlikely there'll be a major problem.) The one plant that drives them mad is rue. If you've got sensitive skin and crash into a clump you'll end up with a gruesome rash.

Not as bad as some tropical whammers mind. *Euphorbia desmondii* can blind you, some nettles produce symptoms like snake bites, and *Antiaris toxicaria* is *the* poison for toxic arrows. Kings of Java used to kill their unfaithful concubines by cutting their breasts and inserting the latex. They died in a couple of minutes. And that's before you get to the poisonous mushrooms and death cap (*Amanita phalloides*) which is the highest-ranking fungus killer in the UK. Just 5–7mg is enough to kill an adult, and each fresh *phalloides* is packed with double that. Get past its smell (like a sprouting potato), and they'll be dryness in the mouth, then the fireworks. Violent vomiting and diarrhoea. The battering continues with hallucinations and convulsions. If the extreme kidney and liver damage doesn't kill you, heart failure will.

To get a full list of "potentially harmful" plants (compiled in 2000 by The Horticultural Trades Association, Guy's & St Thomas' Poisons Information Service and the Royal Botanic Gardens, Kew), visit *www.kew.org/science/ecbot/HTA_ code_list.pdf*. It provides three categories of such plants, with eight in Category A, 33 in B and 81 in C (but how many people eat a wisteria?), though you'll only encounter many in botanical gardens. As for mushrooms. Go to Waitrose. Don't risk it.

7

GARDENING ON THE (ALMOST) CHEAP

First, get a decent batch of tools. Besides a lawnmower – forget the school fees, buy the most expensive lawnmower for your size garden and it'll last 10 years plus; don't waste your money on one of those cheapo-crapo things from a super-market – you'll need a . . .

- hand fork and trowel – wrap bright red electric tape around the handles or you'll immediately lose them; manufacturers always idiotically camouflage them in brown or green.

- border fork and spade – builder's merchants sell virtually indestructible spades but if you're trying to dig out roots like a rhino's neck don't keep forcing the shaft right back because it'll snap.

- secateurs – get the bypass or parrot kind which cut like scissors, and not the anvil sort when one blade chops straight down onto another. Throw money at a good pair and get them sharpened each winter. Some manufacturers run their own repair service.

- shears – for trimming shortish lengths of hedge and tufts of long grass which you can't reach with the lawnmower. Get them sharpened annually. Unless you need . . .

- hedge trimmers – for bigger hedges. If buying the electric kind you must plug it into a circuit breaker or RCD adaptor, which immediately shuts off the supply if you cut through the wire. The petrol-driven kind are heavy, powerful, serious pieces of equipment; leave to the professionals. The simplest trimmers come with a rechargeable battery but can be a bit feeble.

- pruning saw – small, viciously sharp with blades about 15–30cm (6–12in) long. Excellent for sawing through narrowish branches.

- loppers – not completely necessary if you've got a good pruning saw, but they chomp through the narrower branches.

- rake – for getting up windfall apples and leaves, etc.

- soil rake – for flattening beds, getting out flints and stones, and smashing down on lumps of clay to break them up.

- wheelbarrow – forget the expensive fancy-pants kind from garden centres. Buy from a builder's merchant.

- gardening gloves – try before buying. Must be supple and thick enough to stop you getting stabbed by a killer berberis.

- hosepipe – double-check what length you need.

- watering can with a fine rose spray – some cans come with large holes which bomb seedlings with crushing great big droplets. Avoid, or buy sprayers, say two large . . .

- outdoor water sprayers – the 5 litre size – with an adjustable fine/water jet spray. One sprayer is essential for chemical spraying outdoor tomatoes against blight – and YES you've got to do it – or plants might be crippled by an incurable outbreak of multiplying brown patches on the stems and leaves, which then rot and demolish the fruit, and the whole plant is a total right-off. The second is good for gently watering the likes of seedlings. Which brings us to the last buy . . .

- rootrainers – sow your seeds in these. I could describe them but just look at *www.rootrainers.co.uk*. Fill the compartments with multipurpose compost with added vermiculite/perlite, and then start sowing. The roots are forced to grow straight down, so you get a nice long batch, and that beats growing them in small pots/trays and having to keep moving them/forking them into bigger pots. When you see the roots start poking out of the bottom of the trainers, just snap open the compartments and take out the plugs and plant. That said, people have been using small pots or seedtrays for aeons. Take your pick.

DIY propagation
Plants propagate themselves in the wild and they're no different from the rest of us. When they want to score, they slap on the hair gel and tart themselves up with flowers. They want a male, a pollinator, something to transfer the pollen, what Steve Jones calls a 'flying penis'. The flashiest flowers giving the best supply of nectar get most punters. Some flowers are all mouth, and trick potential partners into rummaging around their innards. Dancing lady orchids (*Oncidium*) produce flowers which look like an army of bees; when the real bees see them they charge and attack and brush against the pollen. Job done. What you're going to do is sidestep all these shenanigans so that propagation happens when and where you want. So . . .

- Grow more of a favourite plant and save a fortune.

• Grow replacements when one is clapped out.
• Grow a younger version when the old is getting too big and straggly.

There are four basic techniques, but knowing three is fine. You don't need a greenhouse, special tools or brain. First . . .

Sowing
That usually means annuals and vegetables. You sow in spring, indoors or out. Doing it outside sounds fine, but everything that moves out-there is a psychopathic killer, ie pigeons, slugs, cats, mice and children. If you find a stack of old supermarket baskets, they're very effective turned upside down over seedlings, though that won't keep out soft, succulent exploding slugs (see pages 170–4). Have you ever stamped on one bare foot? Like a cold wet bursting slimy sausage.

1. If you're sowing seed indoors and you don't have a cold frame (see pages 129–30), ie a holding zone, a mid-way stage between being stuck indoors and unleashed outside, where plants get acclimatized to the weather, you must not start sowing until a few weeks before the seedlings can be safely left out, which probably means mid-spring. (The outside weather doesn't just mean daytime temperatures. You go out buck-naked at 3am. See how your seedlings feel.) Sow too many too soon, and where can you keep them? How many windowsills have you got? And how good is the light there? Not very. Which means they'll grow thin and straggly.

2. Fill your containers with multipurpose compost (buy the peat-free kind and maybe they'll stop digging it up), and mix in one part vermiculite or perlite to three parts compost. That improves the drainage. Or just use seed compost.

3. If you've got a greenhouse, get a length of guttering (good

for lettuces) and drill some drainage holes in the bottom. Then half fill with compost (that's the depth, not the length) and sow in that at the right spacing. When the seedlings are the right size, the lengths of the soil-cum-seedlings can be slid straight into long shallows in the ground.

4. If the bag of compost has been standing outside and is cold, put some in a carrier bag and keep indoors for a few days to warm it up.

5. Label the container or you'll forget what's growing where, and give a light drench with a fine rose spray and warm water.

6. The spaced-out large seeds need to be poked in (use a pencil) just under the soil, but if you bury the finest seed, more like dust, it won't always germinate at that depth because it's not getting enough light. So miniscule seed lies on the surface.

7. When scattering the finest you invariably end up with such dense clusters that the seedlings fail and die. They're packed too close together. So space them out by mixing the fine seed with sand, putting that on a sheet of paper. Fold it in two, and scatter/slide the seed-cum-sand mix down the fold from a height of about 15cm (6in). In general, seed should be covered by its own depth. The compost which covers the fine seed must be scattered on through a sieve to get rid of the lumps. Or just add a layer of vermiculite/perlite which lets in light.

8. Then put the container in a clear plastic bag. Stick that in an airing cupboard at about 18°C (65°F); do not blast with heat. This generates warmth and humidity. Keep wiping off the condensation, and get rid of the bag the moment the shoots appear.

9. Now stand on a bright windowsill but not in scorching sun. Keep turning so the seedlings don't produce one-directional growth to the light.

10. Seedlings being grown in small mini pots and trays will eventually need moving to slightly larger individual containers, giving them more side and root space to grow, unless it's time to plant them straight out. Don't move up a size when the seedlings have developed their first rounded set of leaves, wait for their second different kind of leaves. Again use multipurpose compost, but this time without the vermiculite/perlite. Again, keep turning the pots to the light. If the plants are being kept in multi-purpose for more than six weeks, start using a weak all-purpose plant feed because there won't be any fertilizer left in the compost.

11. Gently brushing your hand over the seedlings produces slightly sturdier plants, just as trees grown outside – where they're blown about by the wind – are better than their weedier counterparts growing in a huge glasshouse.

12. Keep moving into slightly larger pots, as the roots fill the old ones. When plants don't need such cosseting, stand out in a cold frame or in a bright, sheltered spot (at the base of a hedge) on good days and bring in for safety at night. Stick with this regime until they look ready for planting out and the weather forecast guarantees benign conditions. Don't stand them out the night before the French fling rainstorms across the Channel.

13. Nip out the tops of young flowering plants and they'll develop lots of replacement (bushy) growth giving extra flowers and fruit.

BUT . . .

1. If you are sowing direct outside, make sure that the site has been well-weeded, and chuck out pebbles and stones which might get raked onto and squash the seedlings. Rake the soil again and again and again, smashing any clods into a zillion pieces with the back of a rake. Level the site and don't start sowing until . . .

2. The soil is warm enough. Hardy plants need it to stay above 9°C (48°F), half-hardy plants above 16–18°C (60–65°F), and don't even think about sowing tender plants until late spring or early summer. Don't be fooled by one spanking hot spring day.

3. And check you're sowing where the plants will be happy, so investigate what conditions they need, ranging from gloomy shade to plutonium meltdown.

4. And while they've got baby roots, only give them a fine sprinkling of water when the topsoil is dry and don't blast them with boulder-like drops.

5. When you get a mini-forest of seedlings, thin them out or they'll be permanently crammed, fighting for survival, food, water and space, and definitely more prone to disease.

6. But if all this sounds a bit much . . .

Take cuttings
Snip off the top of a non-flowering stem, stick it in a pot of multipurpose compost and you've got a new plant. To be more precise . . .

1. Only use a healthy alpha parent, and take cuttings in early

Fig. 13a. How to take a cutting.

summer. You can do it earlier and later, even in autumn, but now gives good results and time for it to make a decent young plant.

2. Always take the cutting – about 10cm (4in) long – just above the place where a leaf stalk joins the stem (Fig. 13a). Then hold the cutting and slice off the bottom length of stem; make this second cut (Fig. 13b) just below where the bottom leaf joins the stem.

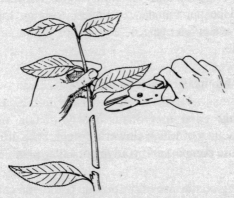

Fig. 13b. And then trim it off.

3. Remove the lower leaves.

4. Lightly dab a bit of rooting powder on the end of the cut stem, and stick in a small pot with multipurpose compost, aiming for say three cuttings around the edge of an 8cm (3in) plastic pot. Water gently.

5. You can put this in a clear plastic bag for extra humidity, keeping the roof clear of the top leaves using a stick and wipe off the condensation, but it isn't absolutely necessary when you've taken cuttings which are quite firm (eg pelargoniums). The soft ones do need protection. Stand in a bright place and keep turning to the light.

6. As they start putting on growth, remove the tent and eventually acclimatize to life outside.

7. Young plants might not survive their first winter outside, especially if the ground stays cold and wet. Repot in late autumn and keep in a cold frame until next spring.

But if the parent plant is rather ropy?
Or you need a multitude of cuttings, cut the plant back to make it produce an abundance of decent new growth and use them for cuttings next year.

Or try dividing
An established plant which is a decent size can be cut into several portions, a bit like a cake, but each must have a section of roots and good topgrowth. Newly bought plants can immediately be divided, giving say three for the price of one, while those in the garden can be dug up. The best time? Early spring.

Depending on the size of the dug-up plant, you can (1) with small, manageable clumps, tear each apart by hand or slice into sections with a knife or (2) with large chunks, divide them with a spade or two forks. Insert the first fork into the clump, then the second to the same depth, so that they're back-to-back. Shove them in opposite directions, tearing the clump in two. That's what they say in the books but it's rarely that simple, and might take two Desperate Dans and quite a bit of rocking to and fro; big sections can be further subdivided. The new sections go straight back into the ground, at the same planting depth as before. Mix some compost into the excavated soil, and pack it in around the roots. Water in well. Try and do this before days of heavy rain so that they don't dry out.

A lot of plants naturally create a large clump, and die out in the centre. They gradually increase outwards from there. That's fine in nature but looks pretty ghastly in a border. The moment you see it happening, divide. Use the younger, more virile outer sections and get rid of the gappy chunks near the centre. They're no good.

Suckers

Some shrubs and trees regenerate themselves by sending up new shoots or suckers from their roots, or an underground section of stem. Some you want, some not.

First, the suckers from shrubs which are basically two plants fused together (eg most roses). They've got the roots of one plant and the topgrowth of another. Why? Nurserymen want the sell-able fancy flowers on one plant but aren't impressed by its vigour, its engine, the roots, so they replace them with the roots from a more virile plant. Well you don't want the suckers from one of these plants because they'll give a different kind of flower. So just scrape back the soil to expose the join and tug the sucker away; never cut it off because that just leaves behind dormant buds and you'll perpetuate the problem. But when plants which haven't been customized produce suckers . . . aha . . . cut them off and use as cuttings.

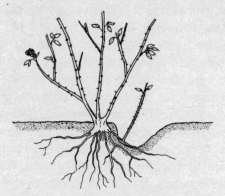

Fig. 14. How to remove an unwanted sucker.

Scrape back the soil to where the sucker emerges (Fig. 14), and see if it has produced its own set of roots. If not, wait. When there's a good batch, remove the sucker first where it joins the parent, and then just below its own set of roots. This can now be planted somewhere else in the garden, unless you want an expanding colony of shrubs, in which case let the plants get on with it.

Layering

Lots of plants in the wild produce lengths of stem which flop across the soil, and they eventually develop roots where they touch the ground. You can use them as new plants. Blackberries and strawberries do it. All layering involves is copying nature with a bit of fine-tuning.

Take a long, supple length of stem (from a magnolia or rhododendron, for example) bend it to the ground and lie it down. Now work back from the last stage. You want to leave the last 15cm (6in) of stem poking out of the ground (Fig. 15), that's the tip of the new plant, so mark that off. Some 10cm (4in) before that is where it'll root, just below where a leaf stalk joins the stem. Mark the ground. Now weed the area, add well-rotted compost if necessary and dig up the soil, breaking up any clods. The soil has got to be crumbly and free draining.

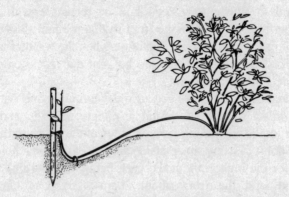

Fig. 15. How to layer a stem.

Use another site if the ground is very poor. Then dig the 15cm (6in) deep planting hole and make sure that the side which is facing the parent plant slopes gradually towards it, with the far side being a vertical. You'll also need to clear the ground 30cm (1ft) around that so that grass and weeds don't get near, competing for moisture and nutrients.

To encourage the stem to root, you can damage it (ie panic it into self-survival). Not badly, just give the stem a little nick with the point of a sharp knife just below where a leaf stalk joins. Then remove the leaves from this section back to the parent, but leave them on the final 15cm (6in). Now peel back a slither of the wounded bark, dab on rooting powder and bend this section into the hole, then up and out the vertical side. Fix the stem in place with an upside down U-piece of galvanized wire. Keep weeding and watering and, after 12 months, check for a good root system. This could take another 12 months, depending on the plant. Then sever from the parent just below its new set of roots and plant out in autumn or spring. Sounds complicated but it isn't.

A cold frame is . . .
an acclimatization chamber where you can stand young plants, getting them used to life outdoors. It's basically a

bottomless sturdy four-sided box or rectangle with a lid sloping from the back to the front so that the rain slashes off; prop it open on good days and close when the weather is bad. Even on bad days it'll need to be kept ajar occasionally to provide some ventilation.

If making your own, get an old window frame with the glass intact for the lid, letting in plenty of light, and then construct the supporting sides. The lower the better so that the walls don't cast any shade inside and it's easy to reach within. Aim for the high point at the back being 45cm (18in) above ground, and the front about 20cm (8in). Use tanalized (preserved) floorboards for the sides. Non-preserved wood will need several annual coats of paint to stop it rotting. If all that is a bit much, then get someone to make one or buy one. Stand it on paving or a well-weeded area covered by weed-suppressant matting covered by a thick layer of pebbles. Keep inspecting for slugs.

8

CONTAINERS

Are they worth it?

If they add shape, colour and fun, yes. But they'll need hefty watering in a hot, dry spell. Compost in the smallest pot dries out incredibly quickly. Who'll spend hours doing the watering when you're holidaying in Zambezi? And while everyone sticks their precious tender plants in pots, where will they go in winter? The roots of that rich blue salvia will just be a few millimetres, the width of the pot's sides, from battering icy winds. Not a good idea. Think ahead.

What makes a good container?

You've a choice of five materials, starting with clay. Plenty of pros – it looks the part, comes in 90cm (3ft) high swagged kinds costing £1,000 as well as midgets for a fiver – but on the downside it can break. It's also quick to dry out but not if you line the insides with polythene liner, making a barrier between the compost and the sides. Do check that the clay is frost-proof (being frost-resistant is NOT good enough). You can paint terracotta pots any colour in stripes, hoops, zigzags and dots, etc. For black and white stripes paint the outside of the pot black, and the top third of the interior. When dry add vertical strips of masking tape. Apply a second all-over colour of white. Remove the strips when dry.

- Old stone pots – when buying haggle like mad because they cost big time – have a patina of lichens and colouration and come in all sorts of fat, wonky, bulging shapes, and though heavy (try lifting one of those filled with wet soil) are worth their weight in gold. Cheap modern copies made from concrete or reconstituted stone can be given a hint of instant antiquity by smearing them with live yogurt, and algae quickly appears. Rural folk can use a mix of cow manure and water but not in Kensington, thank you. Put the large stone and clay kinds in the right position before planting because you'll crack your back if you try shifting them around the garden. And if you don't want them nicked, concrete in place.

- Wooden containers basically mean half-barrels and tubs, big enough for large shrubs (especially camellias which need acid soil), while at the other extreme there's . . .

- Shiny metal, popular with trendy designers needing some-where to stick evergreen box balls and the black-stemmed bamboo (*Phyllostachys nigra*). On scorching days the metal doubles as a frying pan and the roots against the inner walls get frazzled, so again line with polythene. This also stops the compost drying out very quickly. Even better, top it off with hefty handfuls of gravel, seashells or coloured crushed glass and this sets off the plants and helps minimize evaporation.

- The fifth choice is synthetic (plastic, fibreglass, etc) containers, and while not everyone's taste, they are brightly coloured and lightweight, and a good option on balconies but not if you're using top-heavy plants because they'll go flying in the first gale and you'll be done for manslaughter. Also try anything from old Wellington boots to a Mini Cooper.

What next?

All containers must (no option) have drainage holes drilled in the bottom. And anything made of wood, that is intended for long-term use, needs to be treated when clean and dry or it'll rot. Use a wood stain or wood preservative, such as linseed oil, which won't kill the plants. As an extra protection, line the insides with polythene. The internal polythene liner also needs to have drainage holes in the bottom; spear down through it, making holes through the container.

Also clean and scrub all containers, scrupulously, to prize off any baby slugs hiding in the rim and to get rid of pests and diseases. Then fill the bottom with large stones, pieces of old broken clay pots or smashed dinner plates to keep the drainage holes clear and help the water drain quickly away. To minimize the weight, you can use polystyrene chips instead. If growing annuals in large pots, it's a waste of money filling the whole thing with compost when the roots won't go down to the bottom. So fill one-half of the insides with polystyrene chips, then add the compost.

Does it matter what compost you throw in?
There's a basic two-way choice. First, the John Innes composts. John Innes isn't a company, it's a recipe, and these composts – the weak seed compost, the fractionally stronger No. 1 for young seedlings, No. 2 (double the strength) for houseplants and vegetables in pots, and the strongest, richer No. 3 for containerized shrubs and heavy feeders – are called loam- or soil-based. They're not completely peat-free, and the quality isn't a fixed absolute, with some brands giving better results. Gardening magazines periodically do comparisons. Though these composts have a good supply of nutrients, they'll be used up after three months and that's when you have to start feeding.

If using lighter loam- or soilless composts (that's peat, coir and multipurpose), which don't hold the same amount of nutrients, you'll have to start feeding after about five weeks. They dry out quite quickly and aren't a good idea for garden pots. You can also use the compost from new growbags. Take it out and smash it with the back of a trowel to break it up into a crumbly texture. Some brands include 65 per cent peat, so the danger of using that in an outdoor pot is that it'll dry out quite quickly in hot weather, and if you don't keep an eye on it rewetting can be quite a problem. The compost shrinks and leaves gaps all around the edges. Growbag composts have roughly the same nutrient levels as John Innes No. 2 but won't retain it for as long, and again you'll need to start feeding after about five weeks. If John Innes is too heavy a soil, try mixing it 50:50 with growbag compost, but why are you using peat?

The most important paragraph in the whole book.
According to the website of the Royal Botanic Gardens, Kew, (*www.kew.org/ksheets/peat.html*): "In Great Britain, over 94 per cent of the 69,700 ha of peatbogs have been damaged or destroyed. Most of this damage has occurred in the last 50 or so years, since the promotion of large-scale use of peat for the horticultural industry. Peatbogs are important sites for wildlife. They are unique habitats which support a fascinating variety of birds, invertebrates and plants." What are *you* going to do about it?

Watering, feeding, etc
To help minimize the amount of watering in pots, add water-retaining gels when pouring in the compost. It swells out-rageously to many times its own weight with water, and gradually leaches it back into the compost. Quick growers and drinkers benefit most. In any event, water well until the excess drains away. Little and often can be fatal. Slow-release fertil-izer also reduces the amount of feeding you'll do. Scatter in the pellets with the compost.

And, finally, only provide a bigger pot when the roots start poking through the drainage holes, or when the roots are obviously congested. Move up one pot size only. Do this in spring–summer, not autumn–winter.

What if a plant bursts out of its container?
But what did you expect? Plants aren't made to be packed into a tight container. The slow-growers aren't a problem, nor short plants with short roots, but bamboos and *Kniphofia uvaria* 'Nobilis'. Not long-term. So… Start with young plants and keep potting them up, moving them into larger containers, but when that becomes impractical you've got two choices. Cut back the roots and almost bonsai it (adding about 30 per cent new compost), locking and freezing its growth or take a cutting and start again. Take the second option since you'll be using virile new growth, and the old pot plant might well be a bit clapped out. The one advantage of putting plants under stress in a small container is that they're so terrified of dying that they flower even more prolifically to generate more seed and perpetuate the species. A beautiful yelp for help.

Pot plants and ants
Stand a large pot outside on the ground and you're asking for trouble. Sweet-toothed *Lasius* ants march in and the plant looks like it's got the mother of hangovers. You've got to bang it out of the pot. Expose the zillions and zillions of hyped up ants, careering around the roots, and then blast them with ant-powder. Avoidance tactics include standing the pot on an upturned old wire basket, with surrounding plants to hide the base. Or stand the pot on paving where you'll easily spot an invading line of ants heading for the roots of your lemon tree. Or, if it's war, stand the pot on an upturned pot, and then stand that in a tray of water.

Why houseplants belong outside
Because a "houseplant" is an artificial construct. It wasn't designed to sit in a paltry plastic pot on a grubby windowsill in last year's compost being microwaved by the central heating. So give it a break and stand outside over summer, 24/7 when the nights are warm, and it'll perk up. But keep an eye on the watering.

Lemon trees

Yes, you've seen them in Italy. Great big lemon trees erupting fat lemons in fat pots. And everyone says, "You can't grow them in Britain." Well you can. But not oranges. They need 12 warm months.

Citrus 'Verna' sets fruit three times a year and 'Villa Franca' four times, and the excellent French 'Eureka' (or 'Four Seasons') continuously fruits. 'Meyer' is a cross with a mandarin. Tasty and delicious. You can eat the whole thing, skin and all.

From blossom to picking a lemon takes about a year. And the more you pick the ripe lemons the more they'll produce replacement lemons, so don't leave the lemons hanging on. In a 45cm (18in) pot the growth will reach about 1.8m (6ft) high in three years. The pH is very important and needs to be 6.5–7, which is why you mustn't use cement pots. Most specialist nurseries supply their own compost, but if not use John Innes No. 3. Lemons also need an all-year feed (again available from specialist nurseries) and they can be stood outside in summer, being kept cool and humid (the humidity is important, with regular misting) over winter at 10°–13°C. These are not plants for hot, dry living rooms; you'll need a conservatory or frost-free greenhouse. All can be cut back, as and when, to give a better shape. The more ambitious can try Pink and Wheeny grapefruits, Ichangensis Papeda (an ancient Chinese citrus), Sanquinelli and Parson Brown oranges, Hashimoto satsumas, Ellendale tangors, Nagami kumquats, Eustis limequats, and the Kucle (a Sicilian kumquat mandarin).

Other fun container plants include: *Aeonium* 'Zwartkop', *Agave americana* 'Marginata', bananas (*Ensete*), *Begonia luxurians*, brugmansias (eg *B.* x *candida* 'Grand Marnier'), cannas, *Colocasia esculenta* 'Black Magic', *Cosmos atrosanguineus*, *Datura inoxia*, *Eriobotrya japonica*, *Geranium maderense*, *Lilium* Citronella Group, *Opuntia robusta*, *Pennisetum setaceum* 'Rubrum' and salvias (for the richest reds and blues).

Ponds in containers

Large containers can also be used to make mini ponds. Wooden barrels are obvious. If they leak use a sealant, or line the insides with pond liner and staple to the rim. Alternatively make a large rectangular container, about waist high, using hothouse Mexican patterned tiles on the insides and outside, with a wide edge for sitting on.

Don't let children choose the plants because they'll ignore their spread, and you need highly restrained growers. The upright asparagus-like horsetail (*Equisetum hyemale*) has fresh green hollow stems and highly distinctive banding. If the container becomes congested, divide the plant in two (but do keep it in a container because it will spread). Survives being locked in ice. The tiny 'Pygmy' waterlilies (*Nymphaea*) have a small spread of 40cm (16in) and include the yellow 'Helvola' and red 'Rubra'. What was 'Alba' is now *N. teragona*. *N. odorata* var. *minor* is another mini white. Also try everything from the shocking red *Lobelia cardinalis* (best grown in water where it's safe from slugs; plant out in the garden over winter), *Butomus umbellatus*, *Iris ensata*, *Lythrum salicaria* and even the bizarre little *Pistia stratiotes*, like mini floating cabbages with crinkly, spongy leaves. *P. s.* 'Aqua Velvet' is smaller, and 'Ruffles' just 10cm (4in) high and wide, but you'll have to Google an American nursery.

9

KITCHEN GARDENS

Narrow, raised beds
You're NOT allowed to stand on the soil and damage the structure, so the width of the vegetable beds depends on your reach. Stand on one side of the proposed site, reach in and imagine you're poking around, weeding and digging up. Total width is usually about 1.3m (4½ft). Next plan the length, and don't make the beds so long that walking around them drives you bonkers every time you want to get to the other side. Also check that the paths around the beds can take a wheelbarrow. That's the dimension sorted.

But why raised beds? They make a big difference practically and aesthetically because (1) they warm up quicker than those flush with the ground, meaning you can start sowing slightly earlier, getting crops more quickly, (2) forking in extra well-rotted compost to build up the height improves the drainage and (3) there's less bending. However Nos. 1 and 2 do mean that the soil dries out relatively quickly, necessitating extra watering on summer evenings. (4) Putting attractive/ornamental mini walls around the veg. beds also turns them into a very decent feature. Use logs, tanalized timber (painted say green, red or blue), or railway sleepers but they are very wide and mega heavy; also frost-proof bricks (mortar-bonded) or Victorian tiles.

Warming the soil

If you can't wait to start sowing, you'll have to warm up the soil. It's pointless sowing when the ground is so cold and wet that the seed will rot. Hardy seed goes in first when the temperature stays above 9°C (48°F), and the tender when it's above 16°C (60°F), ie at the start of summer. First, though, check that your soil is capable of being warmed up, and that rules out clumpy-lumpy clay. And soil with hefty doses of moisture-retaining organic matter might be too damp.

You can lay plastic sheets on the ground for eight weeks, weighed down with rocks and rubble and planks along the edges, and this might mean you can start sowing four weeks earlier. When the seedlings emerge, they can then be covered by fleece to protect them against cold winds. Alternatively, start sowing seed in root trainers in a greenhouse, perhaps using lengths of guttering for the likes of lettuces (see pages 121–2) in mid-spring so that the moment the outside temperatures pick up they can go straight in the ground at the right spacings, and there's no need for thinning. But the best solution is to buy a large polytunnel so that most of the kitchen garden is under cover (but "under cover" = no rain = *you're* doing the watering), or grow thick evergreen hedges/build stone walls right around the site to block out cold winds and create a warm, still, sheltered microclimate. That makes an amazing difference.

Warm walls

Encircling high stone or brick walls are a Godsend. They create a sheltered patch of ground, and if you want to grow pears like 'Doyenne du Comice' and 'Williams Bon Cretin' they'll need the extra bouncing-back warmth off the wall to ripen the crop. But with the plants' roots in the rain shadow at the foot of the wall, you'll need to get out the hosepipe. Growing against a wall also means you can train the fruit in various patterned ways, not just for aesthetics but to maximize the crop. Try oblique, double or multi cordons, step-over cordons with horizontal branches just above the ground – creating a kind of fruiting mini-fence around a vegetable plot or edging for the length of a path – espaliers and fans. If you want a fancy shape, buy one ready-trained.

(Some) essential crops
Seed packets give all the failsafe stick-it-in-the-ground-2in-deep kind of info, and the companies have got helplines, but it's also worth knowing . . .

Asparagus – has got a shortish cropping season, eight weeks except for the first year (when it's six weeks), but plants should crop for a good 20 years giving 10 or 11 spears a year. Crop every spear (even the weediest) because that will stimulate the dormant buds for next year. Buy the more productive all-male F1 hybrids and plant young crowns on top of a 10cm (4in) high ridge running down the middle of a 30cm (12in) wide trench, that's 15cm (6in) deep. They are spaced out every 45cm (18in). Fill the trench just leaving the plant tips showing. A parallel ridge, in the next trench, must be 45cm (18in) distance from the first ridge. Not for the smallest veg. patch.

Carrots – you need (1) very thin, crumbly soil because if the carrot hits lumpy ground or stones it'll become stunted, so get that right. (2) The big enemy is the carrot fly, so always thin congested seedlings in the evening when the flies are less active, but (3) it'll attack the next day so be ready to erect a 50cm (20in) high barrier of agricultural fleece right around the crop. You can try growing adjacent strongly scented flowers as a distraction but the flies won't fall for that. They're not thick. They're *Carrot Flies*.

Chillies – the range of heat is staggering, from nukes to ticklers. The *Guinness Book of Records* said that the world's hottest chilli was a Red Savina haberno with 57,000 on the

Scoville heat-measuring scale (which measures the capsaicin chemical contents). Pure capsaicin can hit 15–16 million, with US police pepper sprays at 5 million, the Scotch Bonnet at 100,000–325,000, a Jalapeno at 2,500–8,000 and a super-market bell pepper at a puny 0. Then in 2006 came the Dorset Naga, at 923,000 units, from a plant in Bangladesh. *The Times* quoted Aktar Miha, from the Indus Bangladeshi restaurant in Bournemouth, saying that even in its home country this chilli was treated with kid gloves. (Well you wouldn't want to handle *that*.) "It is used in some cooking, mainly with fish curries, but most people don't cook with it. They hold it by the stalk and just touch their food with it . . . It's a killer chilli and you have to be careful and wash your hands and the cutting board. If you don't know what you are doing it could blow your head off." It's worth adding that the growing conditions can be quite an influence. Grow it in Milton Keynes and it won't be quite so lethal.

Google a catalogue from a specialist chilli seed company in the UK and there's a range of some 70 different kinds from the mild to the tonsil-toasters. Step inside a chilli greenhouse (like the one at West Dean Gardens in West Sussex, where they hold a chilli festival each summer) and you're zapped by a Kandinsky flash of reds, blacks, yellows, orange, purple balls, squiggles and curly-wurlies, some nearly 30cm (12in) long. Most chillies start green and turn red. Easy to grow on a windowsill. Use 20cm (8in) pots (larger if possible), water a little and often and cut back the main stem to 45cm (18in) high or lower to make them bushier and get a bigger crop. Provide a high nitrogen feed initially, to promote a good framework of stems and branches, followed by a tomato food for a good crop. The more you pick, the more they'll fruit. Spray with water all over and under the leaves to ward off red spider mites which love the hot, dry conditions indoors. Try keeping plants over winter. Cut back the long branches and keep in a cool room, with minimum watering to keep them just alive. Next year they'll shoot out and be even more productive. And whenever you've sliced open a chilli to get rid of the hot seeds and membrane around them, wash your hands afterwards, especially if you're going to have a yodelling good scratch down *there*.

Courgettes – don't sow the seed until late spring because shoots ping out of the pot, and they're soon ready to go out in the garden. Each plant needs an area 90cm (3ft) square. If some fruit doesn't set, you need to improve the pollination by snipping off a male flower and dabbing it against a female. The females have the young fruit right behind them. Save the flowers and add to salads.

Garlic – just separate the bulbs and stick them in the ground with the flat base plate going in first, the pointy top nearest the surface, 2.5cm (1in) deep. Plant late autumn because it needs a good winter chilling. Ready next summer when the foliage yellows. Spread on wire racks in the sun to dry. Buy bulbs from a specialist supplier. You can buy plump fatties from Waitrose, but those varieties might not grow well in your garden. Specialist suppliers offer about eight different kinds. You could try planting them near carrots to distract the carrot flies.

Leeks – sow the seed indoors in late winter/early spring for putting into a cold frame and planting out in mid-spring/early summer. Scatter wide apart. They'll all germinate. When they're pencil-thick use the end of a broomstick to make 15cm (6in) deep holes about 5cm (2in) wide. Plant one per hole but do NOT fill in with soil. That'll gradually tumble in over the weeks. But do water. In summer mound the soil up around the shafts for long white stems.

Lettuces – sow and go but keep inspecting closely for slugs. Leave one lettuce to bolt (ie go to seed) and it'll spiral up, a skyscraper with bitter leaves.

Potatoes – whack plenty of well-rotted compost into the ground the previous autumn. Buy virus-free seed potatoes, and sit them in compartmentalized egg boxes, letting the tiny buds break and shoot up. Start planting from spring. They go into shallow 13cm (5in) deep trenches about 35cm (14in) apart. Keep covering the shoots as they break through the surface or you'll get a toxic green crop.

Runner beans – you need a netted growing frame to grow them up because each bean shoots a good 2.7m (9ft) high, unless you're growing the dwarf kind. Or make a sturdy wigwam with rods of silver birch or hazel (see pages 49–50), standing the poles 30cm (12in) apart. Make sure that the lowest horizontal arms are about 2.5cm (1in) above ground level so that the young shoots can immediately cling onto the structure. Check that all sides get the sun. Put two beans in the ground at the foot of each rod, and whip out the weakest growth. They germinate very quickly once the soil has warmed up. The more you pick, the larger the crop.

Sweet corn – if you only grow one crop, this is it. Especially the F1 Extra Tender and Sweet (from Thompson & Morgan) which gives two cobs per stem and the sweetest, crunchiest kernels. Just watching them fatten in their sheaths is ecstasy. But you must plant the corn in blocks because they are wind-, not insect-, pollinated. If they're set out across the garden there's little chance that the pollen will be blown from one to the other. Grow 45cm (18in) apart and water well as the kernels are developing. Pray for a long hot summer and pick when a pricked kernel bleeds a milky liquid.

Tomatoes – the best place is a greenhouse or polytunnel where the fruit on a cordon will keep on ripening into autumn, even when the outside weather is foul. You'll get a bigger crop and a longer season. If you've got to grow them outside, no matter.

You'll still get a decent crop until the plants get zapped by the weather.

Cordons grow upright and need to be tied to a sturdy support, whether that's a tall, stout cane firmly and deeply wedged in the ground or a piece of string tied to the roof of the greenhouse/polytunnel at one end and around an iron weight on the ground at the other, by the plant's base. You need to keep pinching out the sideshoots that develop in the "armpit" between stem and leaf, and cut off the top of the plant when it has produced five or six trusses (ie batches of tomatoes) when growing under glass. When outside don't expect more than four to five trusses to ripen, and grow plants in large plastic pots (try buying them from tree nurseries) about 50cm wide x 40cm tall (20 x 16in).

Bush tomatoes are very different. They make shortish, floppy, horizontal growth and fruit all in one go, giving one great glut. Tie the stem loosely to a 90cm (3ft) high cane. You don't need to (indeed couldn't, they're so bushy) pluck the armpits. Bush tomatoes are less trouble, but the trouble is all the fun. Grow cordons. And there's a bigger choice. If you're growing one in a pot/hanging basket, go for 'Red Alert'. And one last tip: when moving a young tomato plant into a bigger pot, always plant it slightly *deeper* than before, right up to the first pair of branches because it'll put out more roots from the low stem. Also spray mature plants (especially the outdoor kind) regularly over summer against blight. It can drive you completely bonkers when amazingly productive plants barnacled with fruit suddenly get hit by blight (and it's devastating in wet summers). Brown patches break out on the stems and leaves and then the fruit rots. Once it strikes there's no stopping it. You must take preventative action.

Intercropping
Some crops take a while to grow, which means that the empty gaps around each developing plant can be used by quick-

growing crops. Leeks take weeks to build up, so plant the likes of rocket and packets of mixed salad leaves in between.

Why crop rotation matters

This is very simple. It's a bad idea to keep growing the same kind of vegetables on the same site year after year because pests and diseases can't believe their luck and move in. So the aim is to keep moving the crops (divided into groups by family *and* growing need, which is why the closely related tomatoes and potatoes aren't in the same bed) around the garden: year one here, year two there, year three in the next bed, then back to the first one. If you've got a spare 10-acre kitchen garden, fine. The roots (basically carrots, leeks, onions and potatoes) are followed by the legumes (beans, courgettes, cucumbers, peas, sweetcorn and tomatoes), and the next year by the brassicas (broccoli, Brussels sprouts, cabbage, cauliflower, radishes, swedes and turnips). The reason for growing the peas and beans in a bed before growing the brassicas is that the former increase the nitrogen content of the soil on which the latter thrive. But if you haven't got three beds, then just grow each crop in a different part of the bed each year. Just remember you mustn't add manure to the root bed within six months of growing crops or they'll fork. And because it's impossible to keep moving a large metal netted frame for climbing beans, just dig up the topsoil at the base and replace it with topsoil from another part of the garden each autumn. And everything should be hunky-dory.

Fruit in the small garden

Because few people have room for full-sized fruit trees, they're available in various sizes. And the sizes are determined by the vigour of the roots which have been grafted beneath the top part which gives the different kinds of fruit. The root is a bit like the engine, and just as you have 900cc and 2.8 litre cars, so apple trees can have different engines (or roots). M27 gives a height of 1.2–1.8m (4–6ft), M9 1.8–2.4m (6–8ft) and M26 2.4–3m

(8–10ft), followed by the taller MM106 and MM111. M26 is generally a better bet than M27 and M9 which can be a bit weedy, but get advice from a specialist nurseryman. And if the soil is poor, then use a more vigorous tree to compensate for the poor growth. Apples aren't self-fertile and need a nearby compatible cultivar which flowers at the same time. Again, take advice. Also look at combination trees which have several different cross-pollinating cultivars joined (or grafted) together and an extended ripening season as the different apples mature several weeks apart.

Many fruit trees can also be grown in large tubs, a good 40cm (16in) apart, using John Innes No. 3. When the roots start trying to escape from the pot, you'll have to prune them back. Add fresh compost each year.

Some (essential) herbs
As with vegetable gardens, herbs need a highly designed, ornamental area to show them off. Always check their growing conditions because they do vary. The Mediterraneans (eg thyme and marjoram) love free-draining ground and wall-to-wall sun while most of the rest thrive in average soil with decent drainage. An obvious list includes . . .

Basil – grow from seed each year; note the different kinds (Richters in Canada – *www.richters.com* – has 14) including those with purple leaves ('Rubin'), large green ('Neopolitana') and ruffled ('Green Ruffles'), all loved by chefs and slugs. Use the largest, widest pots.

Bay – if you live in areas with low rainfall (eg parts of Somerset, above the Levels) you can grow a huge, thick bay hedge, but if you have cold, lumpy clay soil that stays cold and wet all winter you'll have to grow one of those standard bays in a pot, loved by restaurants in Chelsea. Too naff?

Chives – not if you hate their oniony taste.

Fennel – pack the feathery leaves under a roasting chicken and they develop a completely different nutty taste. Totally delicious. Also essential in flowerbeds giving a fuzzy snapshot of plants behind.

Marjoram/oregano – a good mound of leafy growth. *Origanum vulgare* 'Aureum' has bright greeny-yellowish leaves.

Mint – grow it in a bottomless bucket sunk in the soil or its runners (spreading shoots) get everywhere. As with other herbs, note that nurserymen might well rename that pile of plants which they can't flog as 'Sissinghurst' or 'Chicken-flavoured' mint to make a quick sale.

Parsley (curly and plain leaf) – quickly destroyed by slugs. Grow it in a large bucket and stand on an upturned wire basket, but you'll still need to poke around the packed growth every night and morning because the slugs *still* get in.

Rosemary – whichever kind you grow, the floppers or the uprights, note they can be thinned and pruned to smarten them up.

Thyme (especially the tiny-leaved 'Caraway' thyme which really does taste of caraway). Grow it between paving because it thrives in the reflected heat.

Greenhouses and polytunnels
When you've worked out what size you need, double it and then double that *again*. Both are an expensive one-off neces-sity, and once you start propagating and growing tomatoes under cover you'll want to experiment with more and MORE. Aluminium greenhouses give the best light levels, especially when running from west to east with the sun moving across the southern side, and are the top choice if you're growing

tender crops, and they need the least upkeep; if you're aesthetically precious, go for brick or wood (which is also cheaper to heat in winter).

If heating them to increase the range of plants, use an expensive-to-run electric fan heater giving a good flow of air because paraffin heaters can be a pain, and you'll need to keep ventilating to get rid of the water vapour. The third option is a bottled propane gas-heater, and if you're worried about the bottle running out half-way through a freezing night then get an automatic change-over valve attached to two bottles. Failing that, try mains gas.

Also lag the greenhouse walls and roof with polythene bubble wrap with large bubbles (which should last four years) because they let in much more light than the small-hole kind. If you're buying a new greenhouse, ask about what's called twinwall polycarbonate glazing which has good light and insulation levels, but many won't touch it because they say the cavities eventually fill with water and algae. And don't forget summer shading (either paint the exterior glass with a white wash each spring, getting it off in the autumn, or use exterior roller blinds) with plenty of side ventilation panels and roof vents (automatic and manual) because constant fresh air is vital.

Polytunnels are cheaper than greenhouses, and don't need any foundations, but you will have running costs because the plastic needs replacing every five years or so. They also need internal supports for growing the likes of tomatoes and cucumbers but can be filled with large vegetable borders for getting early and late crops.

To control greenhouse/polytunnel pests you need a battery of biological controls. You release miniscule predators and they eat the enemy. Whitefly are destroyed by *Encarsia formosa*, best released in spring while the whitefly numbers are still relatively low and easily controlled, but if they're struggling then try black ladybirds (*Delphastus catalinae*). Use a range of predators (including parasitic wasps and two-

spot ladybirds) against blackfly and greenfly, while a mite
called *Phytoseiulus persimilis* will gobble up red spider mites
which thrive in hot, dry conditions.

10

GARDENS FOR WILDLIFE

Ponds

Make a big one. The biggest you can. The more room for frogs, newts, leeches and dragonflies the better, and they'll quickly move in. Winter is a good time to get digging because you can part fill the pond with rain, not tap water. Leave the planting until spring.

How big and where? Ideally you need a minimum surface area of about 3.7 sq m (40 sq ft) and a depth of 75cm (2½ft) for a healthy balanced environment and fairly clear water. That's the expert view. But what if you haven't got room? Dig it as wide and as deep as you can, and it ought to be 45cm (18in) deep at some point. Select a quiet site where the wildlife won't be disturbed, where you can grow adjacent clumps of wildflowers and leave the grass quite long, giving plenty of cover. The pond needs about eight hours' sun a day, well clear of trees also because both the deciduous and evergreens will drop leaves in the water. And some trees like laburnum are noxious. Position a large pond near sharp shapes and catch their reflections in the water.

Mark out the pond with a hosepipe. Create a large, irregular shape with inlets. Curves are in, tight angles out. And you'll need an inner shelf ideally 30cm (12in) wide, about 30cm below the surface, or as close to those figures as possible, running round part of the pond, on which to stand the marginal pot plants (they're actually grown in mesh baskets). Start with the flashy red *Lobelia cardinalis* making it safe from slugs which crucify it in the garden (but take the pot out of the pond over winter), and *Equisetum hyemale* var. *affine* with a cluster of vertical green stems and black banding, which can get 1.2m (4ft) high. Part of the pond also needs a near horizontal, flattish sloping side where the frogs and toads can waddle out. Hopping into a steep sided pond is easy; leaping out impossible. You can buy pre-formed rigid ponds to plonk in a hole in the ground but the range is very limited. Don't do it.

The key bit comes after the digging. Get on your hands and knees and inspect every single centimetre of the flat, smooth surface prizing out sharp-tipped weeds and stones with a fork. They'll puncture the lining. Then pad the bottom and sides with a thick protective cover. You can buy ready-made underlay, but magazines and/or old carpet are equally effective.

The big cost is the flexible liner. Butyl is the Rolls Royce choice, usually with a 20-year guarantee. Heavy-duty PVC, with a similar guarantee, is cheaper. Carefully lie it in place. The shallow sloping side needs covering with pebbles and stones. Turn it into a crunching shingles beach, then on with the hose. Fill the pond to the three-quarter-full mark and let the rain do the rest. Trim off the excess liner around the edges leaving a flap and tuck it under large rounded stones or under the soil.

Green soup

New pond water *will* turn green; it's unavoidable because the nutrients in the water warm up. It'll also be a green soup every spring to midsummer before the aquatic plants start absorbing the mineral salts which give rise to the green algae (millions of free-floating, single-cell plants).

Small ponds warm up quite quickly and start filling with blanket weed, like green candy floss, from mid-spring. Haul it out by jabbing a stick in the water and wrap it round. The weed comes out in amazing lengths, often with newts trapped inside, so lie it by the side of the water to let the wildlife escape. If you haul out a frog and the cat grabs it, galloping round the garden with a pair of legs poking out of its mouth, grab the cat and get it out. (Don't ask how, *do it*.) And don't be fooled by the fact that the frog will play dead, looking like it has got *rigor mortis*. Leave it alone and it'll eventually crawl back in. Unless of course it really is dead. (Barbecue time.)

In summer you can scoop out some of the clutter (which always falls in) and sludge at the bottom of the pond to eliminate the nutrients which they release. But don't go OTT. The newts and frogs often like hiding in the bottom, so leave a layer of mud. Fish add to the nutrient problem because they turn their pond (and they need THEIR own separate pond because if you put them in with the frogs they'll gobble up all the spawn) into a great big unflushable toilet. And try not to top up the water levels in summer with tap water because that's packed with more nutrients.

You can try to solve the green problem by adding liquid barley extract to the water (they used to recommend chucking great bales of barley straw into the pond until they realized it was completely bonkers). Other chemicals bind the nutrients together to make them sink, when you'll need a different liquid treatment (usually called something like Sludge Buster) to dissolve it. Alternatively a pond filter will break down the nutrients and clear the water, like a mini sewage system. It comes in two parts – there's a filter in a large box (hide it in the undergrowth next to the pond), linked by an in- and out-pipe to the pump (actually in the pond), which runs on mains electricity. Or use an ultra-violet clarifier (which clears the water) and filter (which tackles the algae) with an electric pump. You can get an all-in-one system for just under £200 but regular maintenance is slightly tricky because you'll have to get it all out of the water.

You can even add short-term colour dyes to the water

(black creates a mirror-like surface but it only masks the green problem, it doesn't get rid of it). The dye reflects the UV light and halts the growth of new algae, but you won't be able to see into the depths. (If are going to use black dye, put the pond near a tree with spring blossom and then you'll get the fallen white petals floating on the black surface.) But this is getting a bit OTT and potentially expensive and if you can create a healthy ecosystem without all these pumps and pipes and gizmos, do it. In short, if you've got fish you will need a permanent solution to get rid of all their pooey nitrogen. Without them, the pond should (eventually) look after itself, given the right plants. And you need to start with oxygenators.

Pond plants
They're doubly useful because they're spawning areas and combat algae, but you'll also need some surface growth (like a restrained water lily which won't take over the pond – *Nymphaea* 'Black Princess' is a gorgeous new deep dark velvet red with a spread of 1.2m/4ft; don't forget to nip off the dead flowers to keep promoting extra batches) to cover at least one-third of the water because the shading helps eliminate algae.

You can easily get by with just two kinds of plant, water soldiers (*Stratiotes aloides*) and *Ceratophyllum*. The former look like pineapple tops, and keep the water clear. They sink to the bottom in winter and rise to the surface in summer, and produce a prodigious number of baby plants at the end of stolons or umbilical cords. When the adults get too big, throw them out, detach the young and let them take over. You'll need an occasional summer cull in smallish ponds because you can end up with a couple of layers of pineapple tops which stops you looking into the depths. Also lob in purifying/oxygenating *Ceratophyllum* with one bunch per 0.09sq m (1sq ft) of water surface (they don't need planting in pots, just weigh them down with a stone) and they'll add different shapes in the depths with their long stems and dark green leaves.

Plants that you never ever want in the pond, or to release into the wild, because they are high-octane growers, swamping everything else, include . . .

Australian swamp stonecrop, sometimes called New Zealand
   pygmy weed (*Crassula helmsii)*
Canadian pond weed (*Elodea canadensis*)
Duckweed (*Lemna minor*)
Fairy fern (*Azolla filiculoides*)
Floating pennywort (*Hydrocotyle ranunculoides*)
Parrot's feather (*Myriophyllum aquaticum*)

The wildlife
Frogs should automatically move in, if not ask your neighbours for some frogspawn. A female frog lays up to 4,000 eggs in March (the timing depends on the weather; they'll wait until it's warm), but only a miniscule fraction (0.25 per cent) survive. They're right at the bottom of the food chain. Newts and fish gobble them down. To make sure some survive the early stages, scoop some spawn into large empty clean bottles, and then stand them in a large container/s filled with your pond water, placed in the shade. Do not use tap water. Wait until the water in the bottles is the same temperature as the water in the new container, then slowly swish them in. Add a couple of small *Stratiotes aloides* and lengths of *Ceratophyllum* to keep the water clear and oxygenated, and because the young tadpoles nibble the leaves. Also feed them with gently boiled lettuce leaves or they might get so hungry they completely devour each other. When they develop back legs they become carnivores. Put them back in the pond and hopefully some, just a few, will survive.

You mightn't think you've got many newts but the moment the tadpoles are swished in heads pop out, licking their lips. Newts torpedo after the tadpoles; go into a feeding frenzy. Snap at each other. They're incredibly vicious; like mini lizards. They'll bite a worm which has fallen into the water, tugging and ripping the flesh. Necks straining. If you're squeamish don't look. Twenty-four hours after the tadpole *fest* everything has quietened down. No newts; no tadpoles. They're all (well mainly the newts) hiding away again, in the mud and the blanket weed. You might think that's it, but next year you'll find five or six young froggies have made it. And when mowing long grass in summer frighten out any froglets. It can get awfully messy.

Toads are nocturnal (frogs veer towards being nocturnal but are still active during the day), fatter and dumpier with about the same survival rate. Amazingly, they can live until they're 40. The wonderful protected Natterjack can instantly camouflage itself by changing skin tone to merge with the background. Twenty tons of toads are killed each year on British roads. When threatened, they puff out their bodies and stretch out their legs, looking even more formidable.

The newts basically come in three kinds, the smooth, the palmate and the fabulous Crested which is an amazing mini monster. It has a 15cm (6in) long warty body, and the males have prehistoric cresting right along the back. Surprisingly, these amphibians are terrestrial for much of summer. They prefer damp long grass, stones and logs where they feed on slugs and insects, and shelter from the sun.

If you're unlucky you'll get a great diving beetle. When you see an olive green shape about 3cm (1¼in) long with a faintly striped back and hooped or banded top part with a yellow underside, get it out. It's a voracious predator, and even its larvae decimate newt eggs and tadpoles, while the adults kill frogs, newts and young fish. They fly at night, seeking new sites, making a noise like an angry wasp trying to get out of a window.

The big event is the birth of a dragonfly. It starts off as a disgustingly evil black scorpion-like creature at the bottom of the pond, feeding and growing, shedding its skins, 10 to 15 times, snatching tadpoles in its pincers. After a couple of years it climbs out of the water, up a plant stem, where it hangs until a long, thin dragonfly slips out of its armour-plated gear. There it stays, incredibly vulnerable, drying its diaphanous wings until it can fly. Incredibly fast, it can take midges and mosquitoes on the wing. (A damselfly has four equal-sized wings and eyes on either side of the head; the dragonfly two unequal wings and eyes which are virtually touching.)

Other pond beasties include pond skaters which eat anything that moves on the surface. They have incredibly sensitive hairs which detect anything that falls into, and disturbs, the water. Immediately they know where it is and even, sometimes, what it is. And if anything tries to eat them they can jump or leg it quick. Water boatmen – immediately obvious because they are propelled by two long legs doubling as oars – also have sensitive hairs which detect prey which may have fallen into the water, but they dive and get their meals under the surface. They kill anything from tadpoles to tiny fish and insects by injecting them with toxic saliva. You might even get a grass snake – up to 1.2m (4ft) long – in the pond.

You know when it's there because all the frogs will be sitting like mini Buddhas on the lawn, too petrified to stay in the water. Keep very still and you'll see the snake's head elegantly break surface, tongue tasting the air. Delicately. By now it's probably got one frog bulging in its throat. You might be able to get the snake out with a net. It'll whizz around the pond edge absolutely terrified, hiding its head behind the smallest stone, thinking it can't be seen when of course there's all that body whizzing along behind. Scoop it out gently but it well might emit a vile, stinking liquid. Once in the net it'll play dead (eyes open, tongue hanging out) so don't think it'll wriggle up the pole and get you. Take it to a safe, damp, overgrown place. Release it too near the pond and it'll be straight back for seconds.

At which point it needs to be stressed that you can't have ponds and toddlers.

Bog gardens

A bog garden has moist soil right through the year where you can grow a huge range of plants from the minis to giants with pappadom leaves. If you haven't got a boggy patch, the easiest way to create one is by siting it right behind a pond but not so incredibly close that the nutrients in the boggy soil get sluiced into the pond, turning the water green.

First, dig the basin-like hole in the ground (Fig. 16 overleaf), say 2.4m (8ft) wide and 60cm (2ft) deep. Heap the excavated soil by the side. Then cover the inside of the hole with plastic sheeting, ping through it with a garden fork at the bottom to create the drainage holes and fill the base with 2.5cm (1in) of gravel. The drainage holes are essential to avoid stagnant conditions. You now need to lie a length of hose pipe punctured with holes, so the water can seep out, but with the end blocked off, along the width of the base, on top of the gravel. Wedge it in place and then cover with another 2.5cm (1in) of gravel. This stops the holes being blocked by soil.

Only the end section of hosepipe is perforated. The length before isn't touched, and this runs up to the surface, to sit several inches above it, near the edge of the bog garden, with a connector so that you can attach it to a length of hose that's attached to the water tap. Now replace all that soil, getting rid of any weeds, and it'll eventually settle down to its original level. Don't be tempted to walk over it and quickly squash it down because you'll do more harm than good. If after a few weeks and regular watering it is still too high, then spade off the excess.

When planting, make sure that the whole area is covered so that there aren't any bare patches of soil exposed to the sun, or they'll dry out. Megalomaniacs can stick to *Gunnera manicata,* a dinosaur of a plant getting 2.5m (8ft) tall and wide with thick, jagged leaves a good 1.5m (5ft) wide on top of long spikey 'poles' which power above head high. Over winter you'll need to protect the fat growth buds, down at soil level, by piling the huge dead leaves on top. Alternatively, try

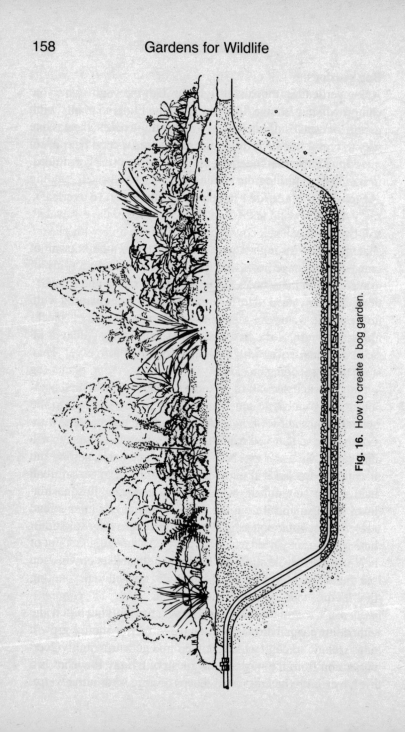

Fig. 16. How to create a bog garden.

the likes of the 1.8m (6ft) high *Ligularia przewalskii* with its great vertical spurts of tiny yellow flowers high above the splayed-finger leaves, *Rodgersia podophylla* – 1.2m (4ft) high – with 40cm (16in) leaves like great satellite dishes and white flowers, and the 2.5m (8ft) high *Rheum palmatum* with 90cm (3ft) long leaves and bursting red flowery eruptions. Primulas, *Iris sibirica* and *I. ensata,* hostas, astilbes and the self-seeding *Angelica archangelica* keep the show alive.

Attracting birds

It's simple. Birds feed on insects so they need a quiet patch of wild ground where spraying is banned for a fresh supply of food, with a mini pond where they can drink and conifers because they keep them alive in winter, and anything with berries to fatten them. Cotoneaster, holly, privet and black-thorn provide generous autumn snacks. Also leave all seedheads in the border. Don't cut anything back.

Starting up from ground level, you want native plants (eg plenty of weeds) and rotting old logs and leaf litter and scuff and muck to attract the insects. Many birds like to peck and scratch at ground level. Also grow evergreen shrubs and trees giving safe nesting sites. Occasionally trim back the growth and plants will send out new bushy replacement growth, and that'll give the birds extra shelter. Their prime winter survival tactic is fluffing out the feathers. This provides more insulation, and a small bird can double its amount of plumage and increase its insulation by 30 per cent. Like even the baldest bird watcher they need excellent cover. An amazing amount of heat can be lost through the beaks and legs. That's why you see birds squatting, immersed in their own duvet, covering their bare spindly legs.

Doesn't sounds much, does it, on those nights when the temperature rips below zero? That's why you should grow a dense tangle of conifers where the birds get surprisingly good protection from icy winds. That mesh of twiggy branches is a life saver. Even bare branches keep roosting birds quite warm.

You can also nail up nest boxes, though there's no guarantee anyone will quickly move in. If one is still empty after a few years, move it to another site or try a different design. Local bird-watching groups give the best advice.

Now let's look at one bird in particular. The miniature goldcrest. An infuriating, obstinate midget.

Europe's smallest bird – it's just 8cm (3½in) long with a wingspan of 15cm (6in), a weight of 6g (0.2oz) and a lifespan of just two to three years – is so small it can apparently get entangled in a spider's web. (You should see the spider.) The mad thing is it doesn't copy other warblers. They migrate to warmer regions in winter but the goldcrest refuses to go. This is bonkers because small birds suffer so much in the cold. Especially when it's freezing. But grow fat conifers (spruces and firs) and it's like building a city with wonky Albanian central heating.

You'd think the goldcrest had signed up for suicide. It could be dying of hunger and it *still* won't touch a bird feeder. It wants insects – a scruffy patch of ground, hedges and thickets. Given shelter and food and you should hear the male's sharp, insistent song, a bit like a high-pitched Mediterranean insect. The *RSPB Complete Birds of Britain and Europe* describes it as a "fast, rhythmic phrase with terminal flourish", like Bach in a trumpety mood, making "*seedli-ee seedli-ee*" sounds, though Robert Burton is closer with his "*si-si-si*" call, and the *Collins Bird Guide* tries to be different with *zree-zree-zree* followed by an "*zezesuzreeo*" as if it's about to escape on a motorbike. Look carefully in the undergrowth and you might spot its yellow flash on the black forehead. Then it'll be out in the open. Add one ivy romping up an old stout tree, a Mecca for insects in autumn, and the goldcrests should survive. Then all you need is a hide.

Building a hide

Hides can be glorified evergreen igloos with a viewing slot or small huts with an old armchair. You can make a terrific one out of lengths of woven growing willow, threaded through taut horizontal wires attached to wooden posts. Set them out in a square, leaving room for an entrance. You can buy the willow online, which usually comes in 2m (6ft) lengths. *Salix viminalis* is your best bet, and grows up to 3.7m (12ft) a year.

Dig a 15cm/6in-wide trench in the ground and get planting. Firmly wedge the willow rods in the ground, 25cm (10in) deep and 30cm (8in) apart. Aim for a criss-cross lattice, weaving them up, over and under a system of horizontal wires hammered to stout posts fixed in the ground. Loosely tie the rods to keep them in place, and then train them to grow across the roof. Nip off the growing points when they're too long. When the hide eventually becomes chock-a-block with new growth, a massive thickening of stems, cut it back in winter and new shoots will quickly sprout out giving new cover.

Alternatively, you can grow a much smarter, more formal hide using box or yew but you won't get instant results because they grow about 30cm (12in) a year. Again you'll need a basic structure using pillars and posts and lengths of taut wire linking them. Line up the box (which is brighter green than yew) about 30cm (12in) apart, and give a regular spring feed of seaweed fertilizer that'll generate strong plants. Keep giving a light all-over trim to force out lots of new, bushy side growth. You can cut out viewing holes by sight or use an old bicycle wheel as a template. If you get it wrong the box will quickly grow over the opening, and you can cut out another hole.

You can also grow climbers up and over an old shed, and even create a green or turf roof by planting it with sedums, wildflowers, grasses and perennials, you name it. First, check that the structure can take a saturated green roof, and that it'll be waterproof (use a waterproof liner over the existing roof). Then fix in place a framework of boards with compartments giving a growing depth of 5–20cm (2–8in). Nail it in place, then fill each compartment with a lightweight substrate, such as crushed brick, and then some compost. Finally, plant up with drought-tolerant plants – and that's essential, unless you want to spend all summer watering your roof. This gives an incredibly natural-looking hide that'll also attract plenty of birds.

If you are putting out food, make it rich in fat. Nuts are an incredible source of energy. Hazelnuts, walnuts and almonds are fine, but always grate peanuts or put them in a wire-mesh feeder so that young birds are forced to chip away and can't swallow them whole. And forget about salted nuts. Also avoid mouldy peanuts because they contain a toxic substance called aflatoxin. You don't want it and nor do the animals. Aflatoxins are often found on nuts, peanuts, dried figs, cereals and spices, and have been linked to liver cancer in some parts of the world. In the European Union there are legal limits to make sure that people don't get infected.

Binoculars

The choice is huge and since they can be incredibly expensive, try different kinds before buying.

When binoculars are listed as 8 x 25, the 8 figure is the magnification and the 25 refers to the diameter of the lens in millimetres. Binoculars with a 10 magnification sound ideal but they won't be small and lightweight. They can weigh 795g, and you try holding that for say 10 minutes without putting them down. Even if you can hold them, your hands will be shaky. And with such a large image and handshake, the image of the bird will bounce around and you'll regret having bought such whoppers. They'll also have a smaller field of view. You're far better off with an 8 magnification lightweight pair for general use, which is easy to carry, and one large magnification pair or a telescope (say 20 plus x 60–80) on a small tripod. The bigger the second figure the more light it lets in, and that's particularly important at dawn and dusk.

Note: don't buy ex-Russian military binoculars for a fiver. They're rubbish. You think our army is badly equipped. Get the most expensive pair you can.

Victimize cats

Cats are the ultimate Janus figure, one minute playing cuddly-wuddly the next trotting out of the undergrowth with a frog in their fangs. Teenage cats are the worst, killing millions of birds a year, especially in spring when the young are at their noisiest, begging for a feed. Don't be surprised to see a teenager making multiple return trips to a nest, laying each post-operation-pink featherless body outside your back door for approval. Last summer I looked up at the magpie nest in the plum tree at the end of the garden, which a pair had taken weeks to build, carting up bits of straw and twig to make a chunky, elaborate home and saw our kitten in it, sitting up, waving back. So how do you keep them out?

If you see one in your garden, run at it singing anything by Queen and it won't come back. (Nor will anyone else.) Or fire a water pistol. Or put a bell on a kitten's collar so that birds can hear it coming. After a few manic years it'll turn into a lazy slob, sleeping in your bed all day, and won't be a serial killer. Also help the birds by growing plenty of long-spined berberis which can shoot up 6m (20ft) high. Once nested up there no cat, thief or giraffe will go anywhere near, even if the nest is packed with a juicy, squishy snack.

The wildlife nobody wants

Thanks to increasing plant imports and the changing climate (a) you can now grow the likes of olive trees in the southern half of the UK while (b) your plants are being flayed to death by Mediterranean invaders and diseases flex their muscles. According to the RHS we've had to cope with 25 new pests in the last 30 years. Look out (especially if you live in the south-east/London/Home Counties area) for the (possibly) invading . . .

Colorado beetle – scampering north, through France, via plants from Spain and Italy. Has a distinctive black and gold striped back and caused havoc to potato crops in the USA. No widespread infestations in Britain and Ireland. Yet . . .

Lily beetle – if it isn't already eating your garden. It disembarked in the 1940s in London and Swansea and had a look round, initially keeping a low profile, but is now a real pest, even in Scotland and Ireland. Immediately obvious because of its scarlet body and black head and legs, it scuttles about chomping mainly through leaves but occasionally flowers and stems (mainly attacking lilies). In extreme cases the leafless bulbs can't store energy for next year, which means in repeated and/or severe cases they might go kaput and stop flowering. Adults appear from late March to May, and they lay rows of eggs on the underside of the leaves. If you're organic, keep picking off and destroying. Sprayers should look for the following chemicals – imidicloprid, acetamiprid and thiacloprid – though what's available keeps changing thanks to the EU.

Pear 'tiger' lacebug – a tiny cream-coloured bug which sucks the leaf sap on pear and apple trees, and in bad cases the foliage loses its dark green colour and falls. Making its way through Europe, into northern France. Related bugs are already in the UK.

Rose jewel beetle – not a rose problem here yet, but it's only a matter of time before they parachute in from northern France. The young burrow into the stems and branches, disrupting the plant's ability to feed.

Rosemary leaf beetle – quite stunning thanks to its green and purple striped body. It arrived from southern Europe and took a while to get used to our rubbish football team and appalling public transport but is now doing very well in the Home Counties and London. Also found on thyme, lavender and species salvias.

Southern green shield bug – quite distinctive with its wide, flat green body and a dark patch near the bum. Comes from southern Europe and is really only a mild nuisance (so far) with beans (French and runners). Mainly found in the south of England.

Termites – related to cockroaches, they shot from southern Spain to France and we've already had one outbreak in the south-west. (In April 2008 the BBC reported that an Indian trader had deposited nearly 700,000 rupees in notes and investment papers in a safe deposit box in the Bank of India, and the lot was had by termites. And no, he didn't get any compensation.)

Pear rust – once a rarity in the UK but no longer. Look out for orange spots on the top of the leaf with corresponding growths beneath. Spray with treatments for pear scab and powdery mildew.

Phytophthora cinnamomi – *Phytophthora* is Greek for 'plant destroyer' and it's paired with *cinnamomi* because the cinnamon tree was one of the first to suffer from this microscopic fungal pathogen. It attacks plants' roots, with yew being high on its list in the UK. From south-east Asia, probably Papua New Guinea. Has caused big problems in the USA.

11

WHAT THEY NEVER TELL YOU

What is life like as a nurseryman?
Miserable, if you're not selling any plants. And it doesn't matter how good the lifestyle, or where you're based, if you haven't got a wealthy partner to bail you out this is high risk . . .

I once interviewed a gardening big wig (who put his name to best-selling, formulaic books) before he (let's say 'A') became famous. (And no, I'm not saying who.) 'A' was highly talented with an exquisite eye for colour. Kind and generous, but was struggling. Hours away from home and the family in a 3-ton truck, doing 20,000 miles a summer, selling first-rate plants at provincial fairs and Hampton Court and doing the Chelsea Flower Show. And if Chelsea sounds high prestige, remember it involves a staggering amount of time planning the display, growing totally immaculate plants which have got to be in flower *that* day, not a second before or after, that's a fat lot of use. And you don't make any money because (a) you can't sell plants (except in the last hour of the last day), (b) you've got to hire helpers (and they'll need paying) because you can't man the stand alone, minute by minute, every day, your ankles swelling up, and (c) you'll all need somewhere to stay, and then (d) while you're away in London, having fun, stalking the celebs on Press Day and marvelling at Ringo Starr's waist – it's about the width of a grapefruit – and how Rod Stewart keeps that shock of grey hair stacked up, not a hair out of place, *who* is running the nursery? And when you do get back and get a 'domestic,' and find your daughter is legging it to Kenya with – where did *he* come from? – and the seedlings have keeled over, guess who wins? Right. The seedlings. All 30,000. Or they'll die. And don't forget: you'll need a clued-up, hands-on partner with a strong back and a deck of brand new credit cards.

And then you need a selling point. You could make a virtue by being off the beaten track, but you'll only get committed customers. Wanting a day out. It's far better being en route to a major attraction, or near a famous garden. Feed off their success. And get plenty of publicity. Crawl to the gardening glossies, the newspapers. Invite someone down. Give an interview. Make it fruity and lively. Tell them you're Ainsley Harriot's love child. You've a DPhil in Discredited Neopythagoreanism. That you know the Duke of Edinburgh's bra size. And once you're on the circuit, other gardening writers (and they're all achingly, gob-smackingly destitute), desperate for something to write about, will start trying to sell you to other publications. Without telling you, of course. While you're also crawling to the gardening photographers (multi millionaires whoofing up and down the motorways in Bugattis) who sell their pix to the media, again doing your job for you. Selling you and your nursery to the glossies *and* the nationals. So you create a self-fulfilling whirlwind of selling *you*.

The gardening industry might be worth around 5.5 *billion* pounds a year (according to pre-Credit Crunch figures from the Horticultural Trade Association), but the average household spends only *c*. £350 p.a. on gardening products, and one-third of that on plants. Most go to the big garden centres which sell everything from pet tarantulas to barbecues with enough power to launch a nuclear missile. So if you're thinking about giving up a job in the city and growing classy plants instead, the big question is . . . can it work?

You'll need (1) to do an RHS propagation course and (2) to

buy a house with enough land for at least two big polytunnels (one for propagating, one for growing) and ideally a show garden, so that people can see what the plants will actually look like. And that in itself is a major, massive achievement. Check the soil, the drainage, the wind. You'll need good quality compost and don't do the one thing you want. Grow amazing rarities. The reason why most plants are rare is nearly always because they're hard to propagate and/or tricky to grow in the garden. Few gardeners have heard of them and even fewer want them. So start by growing big sellers, even if they make you vomit. And most people want easy-grow, colourful/shapely/richly scented plants which don't let up all summer. Attract punters with tasty sweeties and hit them with the smart stuff by the till. Don't hard sell. *Insult them.* ("Would sir like one of these? Ach. No. Perhaps not. So sorry. One does need a rarified eye for *couleur.*" "Whatd'yamean COLOUR. Gimme 10.") And see what sells before stocking up with large numbers. Don't gamble because you'll end up chucking everything over the hedge.

Visit other specialist nurseries in the UK and abroad. Swap. Look out for the next *Cosmos atronsanguineus*, which 20 years ago was a total rarity. Write a catalogue that's an amazing read, like Architectural Plants' tome (that's the West Sussex nursery). Fawn over your customers, like the impeccably nauseating fastidious waiter (John Cleese) tempting Mr Creosote with just "another wafer" in *The Meaning of Life* before his stomach explodes. Or get a reputation as an engaging maniac. Become a major *attraction*. And if driving round the plant fairs all summer, get an air-conditioned van with B&W's computerized hi-fi (the one for the new Jag) with chunky shelves in the back for the plants because when a weak one, packed with pots, goes snap . . .

Become decently successful with say 30 customers a day in summer and you might make £20,000 profit p.a. Of course you won't get rich. But it beats working with a pack of arrogant, self-important, insensitive bankers who spend all their time on rowing machines. And you work by the seasons. In summer up with the geese. Out 'til the first bat appears.

Does that turn you on? Then do it.

Plant hunting

And if all this makes you want to go plant hunting, a few titbits.

About 75 per cent of the typical British garden is an import. Strip out everything from the Far East and beyond and the border will be all bare soil. The Chelsea Flower Show? Chinese Flower Show. That's where nearly everything comes from.

Plant hunting was never easy. In 1910 'Chinese' Wilson went after the Regale lily. His first consignment rotted so he had to go back with his cowboy hat, pet spaniel, a caravan of 25 porters in open-toed sandals, trekking the Great Salt Road, inching down the valley of the Min, a "barren, repelling place" he said. Coming home a rock-fall smashed his foot and he had to lie on a narrow ledge, staring at the sky, with a screaming 300ft drop if he went down, while a mule train marched over him because it couldn't be turned straight back. His porters used the camera tripod as splints, but his leg never really recovered though at least he could boast about his 'lily limp'.

One contemporary plant hunter told me he was once in the Himalayas when he heard a loud bang, turned round, and saw a cow had fallen off a nearby mountain, and splattered right behind him.

Another told me, "I've had to eat bear's paws and gorilla's lips. I remember once being taken into this dingy little cafe, half-way up a mountain. They had all these jars on the shelves and poured one out, and when the owner was putting it back I saw this long curly snake in the liquid. My guide said it'd make me quick!"

So why does everyone go to the Himalayas? Because plants from these high temperate areas tend to be hardy in Britain.

And their forests are packed with terrific plants. There's still a lot to be discovered. Most plant hunters are now sponsored by institutions, but you can go on those trips advertised in gardening mags. One guide told me they're designed to be safe, he can't take any risks, with everything planned in advance but "I tell everyone to bring an umbrella so if they need to go to the loo on a hilltop they can open it up, get behind, and no-one sees a thing."

If you want to go seed gathering you must get prior informed consent through the embassy of the country you're visiting. (Also Google CITES, and look especially at *www.kew.org/conservation/cites-what.html*.) The days of whizzing round the globe treating it like a horticultural super-market are finished. One Roedean-like lady once told me she used to smuggle cuttings back in her knickers. And when getting a seedling back, take Roy Lancaster's tip, and tuck them up in a condom.

Slugs – the real story

First, don't stand on one barefoot. It's like standing in a bowl of last week's spaghetti. Gets squished between your toes. (You've got to scrape it out with a twig while sticking your foot under the hot tap in the kitchen sink. Not as gluey as the adhesive with which a barnacle sticks to a rock, mind, which is nature's toughest, glueiest glue.) And second, before you go hunting slugs at night with a chef's blowtorch, some respect. They're extraordinary, evil *and* disgusting; ie Talented.

One of the biggest slugs in the UK is *Limax cinereoniger,* which can get 30cm (12in) long, with a 50cm (20in) penis when erect. And it's got a European cousin – the same species – with a whirling 90cm (3ft) willie. Both mate upside down while suspended from a plant or branch, dangling by a thread of mucus so they've got room to manoeuvre. Sex can take 24 hours and to keep its partner happy the male's Flying Jimmy is apparently loaded with all kinds of 'gadgets' for inserting and wiggling about.

Most slugs are sequentially hermaphrodites, going from male to female, and have a penis and vagina. In one slug species, when it's all over, instead of having a chat, one slug might chew off the other's penis and swallow it. Even more bizarrely, you'll find a slug's genitalia and anus on the right side of the head, and that means it poops besides its bonce.

Slugs are deaf and often have incredibly bad sight, so they can only just detect light and dark; they have to recognize each other by taste and touch (no joke). Many have evolved romantic rituals to check they're doing it with the right species. They dance. Like us. This way and that, rubbing tummies and licking each other's gunge. You can tell when one's getting randy because the tentacles start to go all droopy (ie the blood's getting sluiced down under).

There are about 29 species in the UK and the quickest wriggle about 12m (40ft) a night. They're territorial and use their mucus/slime trail to find their way back to the same hiding place, which is why you can't leave shady damp sites for them to hide under. Especially when some slugs have 75,000 teeth (other specialist feeders can have 250,000). If you live in South Wales look out for the new ghost slug (*Selenochlamys ysbryda*) which is white with no eyes but has powerful blade-like teeth, sucking up earthworms like noodles.

Slugs are sweet, succulent and glistening. (A slug is a snail which has either lost or reduced its shell, and while slugs are active all year, mainly from April to October, the snails are dormant over winter.) If you've read that they need good supplies of lime to build-up a shell, that's complete rubbish. But not having a shell is a handicap. Dehydration. Slugs avoid this by living in damp areas or only being active at night and after rain. And like snails they pump out a sticky mucus to keep their skin moist and smooth (perhaps that's why Spanish senoritas apparently have a skin cream based on slug slime).

Which reminds me of an ancient cure. Tie a thread through a number of snails' shells and bodies and suspend them over a plate of brown sugar. Their mucilaginous exudations, that's the oozy sticky gunk, drips down. Collect, swish round your mouth and swallow. It (apparently) cures all colds and coughs. You can also use slugs to stem nose bleeds because the slime is very astringent. Just squelch one up your schnoz. You can even rub a live slug over a wart. The Romans did.

But back to chirpy young slugs. You're likely to find the large black slug (*Arion ater*) – also available in orange-brown and buff – and its swashbuckling invading relative *Arion lusitanicus* (from Spain and Portugal) prancing up and down at night. What to do? There's a ghastly insidious nematode called *Phasmarhabditis hermaphrodita* (available from garden centres and by mail order). It kills by searching out slugs and entering via a small pore. This leads to bacterial swelling and blood poisoning. Then the nematode slips out and wipes out victim No. 2. Search and destroy. Water it into the ground in the evenings (and you'll need several applications), but it needs a minimum soil temperature of 5°C (41°F) to work.

Other slug predators include birds, frogs and hedgehogs (attract them with dog food, never milk), though they'll never eradicate the problem. Keep an eye on particularly vulnerable plants, going out at night to skewer slugs with a kebab stick or plop them in a bucket of boiling water or jump up and down and burst them. Sink old jam jars filled with water into the ground, leaving 3cm (1¼in) above ground to stop insects falling in, or scatter halves of scooped out oranges around the garden, and scrape out the slugs each morning. Accidentally leave your carefully nurtured young Jalapeno chilli plant outside overnight and you'll find a monster of a snail glued to the toppled main stem the next morning. (I just did.) It really is up to you.

Particularly vulnerable, wonderful plants can be grown in pots on upturned wire baskets, though some slugs/snails are talented tight-rope walkers, so look out for them. Anti-slug companies keep marketing new weapons, so it's a case of trial and error. There's a new slug mat which has been treated with copper; you spread it on the ground, cutting out a hole for the plants. And there's copper tape for wrapping around a pot, and grease. Scatterings of small, sharp bits of gravel/egg shells/you name it are said to work, but don't waste your time. Toxic slug pellets (varying in toxicity) might be the last resort, but the wildlife may well suffer, say when a frog gulps down a partially infected slug. Time someone invented a slug taser. Otherwise, stick to large-scale gravel gardening under a Mexican sun.

For what it's worth, *Gardener's World* website lists the following plants as being most resistant to slugs, but that doesn't guarantee 100 per cent immunity, especially the tender young growth.

Aquilegias
Astilbes
Astrantias
Begonias
Crocosmias
Euphorbias
Ferns
Fuchsias
Grasses
Hardy geraniums
Hellebores
Hydrangeas
Japanese anemones
Lady's mantle
Lavenders
Pelargoniums
Penstemons
Roses
Sedums

And talking about 'tender', snails are yummy. In southern Spain you can eat snails fattened and sweetened on sugar, then cooked with ham and onions. The French get through 40,000 tons of the common snail (*Helix aspersa*), imported from eastern Europe, but if you want Escargot de Bourgogne you'll need the increasingly hard to find *Helix pomatia*. First, feed them on herbs for seven days, and when they smell delicious they're quickly boiled and simmered. Then poke them back in their shells, add parsley and garlic butter and start sucking. If you need more ideas, Heston Blumenthal – *www.bbc.co.uk/food/recipes/database/snailporridge_74858.s html* – has a snail and porridge recipe using Dijon mustard, Parma ham, sherry and walnut oil, and 72 snails. And the *Independent* – *www.independent.co.uk/life-style/food-and-drink/recipes/rabbit-snail-and-hedgerow-garlic-pie-632146. html* – has a rabbit, snail and hedgerow garlic pie with 12 rabbit legs and 16 snails. Enjoy.

Books, magazines and show gardens. Are they any help?

Or, put another way, who needs them? Take my gardening encyclopedia, a 500-page slab of concrete which reads like it has been written by a committee of constipated tax inspectors which you'll need to load on the back of a great fat sow to get it to the end of the garden, packed with thousands of passport photographs of plants so severely cropped you haven't got a clue what they actually look like. Do you know *how* some of these books are put together? And *who* puts them together? And *who* decides what they look like? Not gardeners.

Art editors, with their brains plugged into an Ipod, who only know about dahlias because of that wonderful ditty "There was a young man from Australia/On his bottom he painted a dahlia . . .", have a major say on the layout, on what looks "sexy", and they create the design, following orders, "Pack in 1,000 plants." "Yessir." Why? Because 1,000 in gold letters sells books. So they find space on each spread to pack in the pix but the teams of criminally underpaid editors – who might well know nothing about gardening – then have a ridiculous job against a crippling deadline deciding which bits of information stay and which bits get cut because there isn't room to say everything which needs to be said. If there's room for just 12 lines of text, 12 lines it is. The rest is cut. And because these books are *so* formulaic and *so* politically correct, and *so* frightened of venturing an opinion – which is precisely what gardening is NOT about – all the juicy titbits, the hows and whys and shortcuts never get mentioned. Which is exactly what you *want*. So if you want to know how to grow anything, get hold of a specialist nurseryman who has been growing the plant for years, and you'll learn more in 10 minutes than from a pile of encyclopedias that we ought to use as bombs against Al Qaeda.

And what about gardening books and magazines, selling on their "inspirational/aspirational" photos, which their marketing men have decided is exactly what we (the readers) need. See it from the photographers' point of view. They're an extraordinary intrepid bunch, willing to drive say 20,000 miles a summer, taking 10,000 snaps, with a frequent four-hour drive to photo a rare beauty of a magnolia which might, and it does happen, get mangled by a storm the night before, or a wind smacks up and the flowers *won't* stay still just when the photographer has set up his equipment and is about to say "SMILE", so the trip down 10 motorways is completely wasted – well they spend their time trying to find new gardens, or new views in old gardens, which have to be photographed *just after dawn* because after that the light is much too hard and harsh.

These pix are bought by editors, who commission a writer to jolly along and write it up. All very good, until you, the writer, get there. And then you discover that the garden bears no relationship to the photos. The photographer wasn't interested in giving a realistic account of the garden, showing the layout and views, how everything links together, but stood in the weirdest places, like on top of a ladder in the swimming pool to get the artiest of arty shots. So what you see are pictures designed to sell to editors, ogling us (the readers) with a pornographic wink. And will editors ever let journalists write what they really think? You must be joking. It's a two-way conspiracy. The writers are paid to ejaculate happy adjectives all over the page.

And show gardens? Forget the fact that some cost half a million, the big problem is that (1) most are designed to be seen from one view only – there, from where you're standing, right in front of them. And (2) they're stuffed with plants which are at their beautified best *right now*. There's no room for plants which flower at other times. So why would anyone copy that? And at the Chelsea Flower Show (even elsewhere) designers have to stick totally to their approved design plan or they won't get a gold . . . If they get mental fizz and suddenly think of an amazing addition half way through building it, they can't do it. Can't change a daisy. They're part judged by exact replication rules which completely eliminate the creative flash. And if that isn't mental . . .

But back to real gardens and the eye-twisters, the comic, the shockers; burst figs, dead ponds and children digging for oil. And maybe, just *maybe*, twice a year, a random miraculous vision. Shimmering instability. Like being electrified in a work of art. Which, after the 180 pages and 50,000 words in this book, the hours I spent at my computer and the moments you slammed it shut screaming, "What are you on ABOUT?", is what gardening is really about. The brain incandescent with magic.

APPENDIX

Nine cheesy plants and TV makeover programmes
Alchemilla mollis – a disgraceful plant that's (a) lime green and insipid, and (b) self-seeds anywhere, even inside a strawberry plant, and you try getting that out.

Skimmia japonica – so prissy and perfect; glossy green leaves and red berries. Belongs in Habitat.

Daffodils – yes I know they come in orange and white, but those yellows. Like some odious medicine from matron that's meant to perk you up. And the looks you get from old ladies when you bribe children to pee on them. I remember going down the Grand Canal in Venice a few years ago and thinking what joy escaping those tedious yellows which splatter gardens like great gobbets of last week's custard and looking up and seeing a window box with yes, a DAFFODIL.

Cortaderia selloana – in front gardens. They're OK at the edge of a field the size of Lancashire but who wants all that galloping, yodelling growth. Totally charmless. Plug it in to the mains. Frazzle it.

Acanthus spinosus – a French poodle of disgustingness.

Fig trees – ie my Black Ischia which (I'm told) originated from a volcanic island in the Bay of Naples. Of course it won't fruit in my clay soil where it's razored by Atlantic gales. What was I doing?

Fuchsias – the ones with those vile vulgar flouncy flowers like 'Swingtime' smacking of ballet lessons with precocious little boys called Niles.

Ferns – what's the point. They don't do anything.

Pointsettia – tarty knicker-red garish flowers (all right, bracts) and millions get sold at Christmas and why would anyone buy one, and why would anyone pretend to be grateful? And they all get chucked out with the rubbish.

Garden makeover programmes – why would anyone ever want to have their garden, their taste and their dreams squandered, belched over and desecrated by these ghastly programmes?

Ten plants to covet

Nepenthes spectabilis – an insect-eating pitcher plant from highland Borneo, growing at over 1000m (3,300ft), a distended mouth frozen open, waiting waiting, at the end of a slinky black pouch.

Gardenia augusta – with a brain-filling scent.

Dahlia 'Norbeck Dusky' – rich wine red magical purple and lots of pointy petals.

Prunus serrula – for the sheer totally overwhelming tactile glossy bark.

Echinopsis hybrid – a spiky fattening rich green cactus with deep channels like ravines running from top to bottom to sluice every last bit of dew down to the base of the plant, giving it a drink. Then unbelievably long asparagus-like stems with tufty black hairs at the base fire out and the engorged heads swell and balloon . . . plumper and plumper until you think they'll explode and then, at about 10 o'clock at night, the most exquisite pale yellow-pink flowers with a deep deep throat open with the softest sweetest scent (switch off the lights and shine a torch inside) and stay open for about 48 hours and then that's it, the flowers collapse, exhausted, wrinkle, shrivel and die. If you have a mature plant there'll be more mini cactuses barnacled around the base and they're all launching their own flowers from May. In the wild they're pollinated by insects, hawkmoths and hummingbirds.

Echium pininana – for the leafy thickets and outrageously tall flower spikes.

Pinus patula – the greenest green of long dangly leaves from branches high in the sky.

Scotch thistle (*Onopordum acanthium*) – a Man's Plant with 2.4m (8ft) of swanky, testosterone growth.

Anchusa azurea 'Loddon Royalist' – the richest most sumptuous blue for early summer. Just when you need it. 90cm (3ft) high.

Eucalyptus viminalis – for the sheer chutzpah; they slide and snake and poke that upthrust into the stratosphere.

The Fibonacci numbers

When Galileo more or less said, "I discovered the book of the universe, written in the language of mathematics," he ought to

have been referring to the Fibonacci sequence of numbers –
1, 1, 2, 3, 5, 8, 13, 21, 34, 55, 89, 144, 233, 377, 610, 987, etc.
They are frequently embedded everywhere, in architecture,
music and nature, from the number of petals on a flower to the
number of spirals on a cauliflower and pine cone. And no it's
not mystic nonsense. Look at *www.maths.surrey.ac.uk/hosted-
sites/R.Knott/Fibonacci* or have a look at pages 513–32 in *In
Our Time* (ed. Melvyn Bragg, Hodder and Stoughton, 2009)
where three boffins explain all.

GENERAL INDEX

PLANT INDEX